GW00949849

JUDAICA

LITERATURE IN THE WAKE OF THE HOLOCAUST

BOOKS BY LEON I. YUDKIN

Isaac Lamdan: A Study in Twentieth Century Hebrew Poetry (London, 1971)

Escape into Siege: A Survey of Israeli Literature Today (London, 1974)

Jewish Writing and Identity in the Twentieth Century (London, 1982)

1948 and After: Aspects of Israeli Fiction (Manchester, 1984)

On the Poetry of Uri Zvi Greenberg [in Hebrew], (Jerusalem, 1987)

Else Lasker-Schüler: A Study in German Jewish Literature (London, 1991)

Beyond Sequence: Current Israeli Fiction and its Context (London, 1992)

A Home Within: Varieties of Jewish Expression in Modern Fiction (London, 1996)

Public Crisis and Literary Response: The Adjustment of Modern Jewish Literature (Paris, 2001)

Edited

Modern Hebrew Literature in English Translation (New York, 1987)

Agnon: Texts and Contexts in English Translation (New York, 1988)

Hebrew Literature in the Wake of the Holocaust (New Jersey, 1993)

Israeli Writers Consider the Outsider (New Jersey, 1993)

Coedited (with Benjamin Tammuz)

Meetings with the Angel: Seven Stories from Israel (London, 1973)

LEON I. YUDKIN

LITERATURE IN THE WAKE OF THE HOLOCAUST

SUGER PRESS
Université Paris VIII
in association with
ejps
THE EUROPEAN JEWISH PUBLICATION SOCIETY

LES EDITIONS SUGER / SUGER PRESS
Université de Paris VIII
15, rue Catulienne, 93200 Saint-Denis, France. Website: www.ieeh.org

in association with
THE EUROPEAN JEWISH PUBLICATION SOCIETY
PO Box 19948, London N3 3ZJ. Website: www.ejps.org.uk

The European Jewish Publication Society is a registered charity, which gives grants to assist in the publication and distribution of books relevant to Jewish literature, history, religion, philosophy, politics, and culture.

© LES EDITIONS SUGER 2003

ISBN 2-912590-21-3

Printed in France
Cover design by: Nelly Sabatier

ACKNOWLEDGEMENTS

Parts of this book have appeared in somewhat different form in the following: *World Literature Today, Holocaust Literature, Directory of Literary Biography: Holocaust Novel*. Inevitably, this material has been recast for the purposes here.

I would like to thank Antony Rudolf, Yehiel Sheintukh and Efraim Sicher for their invaluable and gracious assistance in the preparation of the chapter on Ka-Tzetnik.

I would like to thank the staff of the Université de Paris VIII in the persons of Professors Ephraim Riveline and Gideon Kouts for their encouragement in this project, and for enabling publication. I would particularly like to express my appreciation to Dr. Livia Parnes, for her supremely conscientious and professional editing.

TABLE OF CONTENTS

PREFACE

The Holocaust is arguably the most astonishing episode in modern history. For insane destructiveness, directed cruelty, breadth of scope, extent both geographical and chronological, there has been no equal. The atomic bombs dropped on Hiroshima and Nagasaki were awesome in their effect, the recent civil wars in Africa and Yugoslavia have been gruesome to a degree, the genocide in Cambodia horrific. But the Nazi Holocaust has remained in some respects unique, in its ambition to exterminate a whole people dispersed internationally, rather than just within the theatre of war. But it is also paradigmatic. Certainly, it has taught us much about the potentialities of human nature and behaviour, much of which we would perhaps prefer not to learn.

Literature is the articulate reaction to the Holocaust. For all their inadequacy, words are the most powerful instrument for the representation of the situation of the individual. Through their nuances and subtlety, their precision and their range, they allow us a glimpse of understanding into the souls of perpetrators and victims, bystanders and descendants, as well as of people in general, who must necessarily live forever in the shadow of this cataclysm. That this has happened tells us that it was a product of humanity, that it happened to so many, of such diverse origins, countries and cultures, tells us something of what people are capable of, both good and evil.

Holocaust literature is a phenomenon of enormous range, extent and mode. It covers all genres, languages, and, for that matter, each phase, as all sensitive creativity emanating from beyond World War II, operates in its shadow. Primarily, of course, it is a Jewish concern, as it was specifically against the Jews that the destruction was aimed, and so it is the Jews who must absorb the targeted enmity. By absorbing, they also express interpretation, and give it a form, which in itself is literature. But, equally obviously, it is not solely the concern of the Jews. Since this blast of hatred burst boundaries, it is both a product of all and the business of all. The literary response is universal and international, so the literature described here, one tiny part of the total range in existence, is written in many languages, and covers a wide range of genres. It accompanies the action, reflects on it, and also translates it into other modes. All these strive to find the appropriate garb and the various applications. There can be, and indeed are, many such, ranging from diaries, reporting factually and coolly, to journals, selecting key moments and highlighting them, to fiction, imaginatively extrapolating from the historical material in the direction of a less confined expression. It has not been the purpose of this book to validate one form over another, or to grant exclusive legitimacy to any particular representation rather than its alternative. What we look for is internal consistency and authenticity, the truth of the presented material, as well as the clear preservation of appropriate distinctions between factuality and imaginative reconstruction.

Much valuable work has been devoted to Holocaust literature, and some of it has been taken into account in this modest offering, although all of it has been found useful and enlightening. What I propose here is a description of writing that has emerged from various perspectives, and of the struggle to effect different aims.

I

THE HOLOCAUST AND THE WRITER

The Experience and the Text

To write about the Holocaust is to explore human behaviour at its most extreme. It is also to delve into the subject in literary terms, and to give it a form within the parameters of existing literary tradition. There are no other meaningful options, and we must needs either write about it, or remain silent. This latter, apart from being literally meaningless, is evidently not a literary option. In describing what literature has done with all this horror, and how the writer has treated it, Lawrence Langer, one of the first scholars to treat the material systematically, says of the enterprise that it exists in order: '[t]o explore ways in which the writer has devised an idiom and a style for the unspeakable, and particularly the unspeakable horrors at the heart of the Holocaust experience.'[1] A paradox remains. Literature takes its significance from the pleasure of the text, and yet the subject of this material is utter despair and ultimate pain; it can never match up to the reality that it seeks to

---

[1] Lawrence Langer, *The Holocaust and the Literary Imagination* (New Haven: Yale University Press, 1975), xii.

represent. As Alfred Kazin writes: 'To be a Jew is to know that words strive after the reality but can never adequately capture the human situation.'[2] But, as we are compelled to see, even death has a narrative. Human kind always stays in place, as long as there is a reader and a potential text. Death brings all this to an end, and pain may seem to dwarf all other considerations beyond itself into insignificance. But death is also the subject of the writing; disappearance now comes onto the screen.

Little can be advanced without a consideration of the uniqueness of the Holocaust in human history.[3] Can it be slotted into the template of precedent, or has there not taken place a radical breach with the past? This question is persistently raised, because if the second question be answered in the affirmative, then any sort of mimesis, however faithful, authentic and true, might well become irrelevant: 'Even the most vivid presentation of concrete detail and specificity, the most palpable reconstruction of Holocaust reality, is blunted by the fact that there is no analogue in human experience.'[4] Traditionally, a realist writer, even whilst summoning up a landscape of utter awfulness, would still write in implicit reference to another reality. Any sort of critical view, especially satirical writing, only makes sense within the purview of a

---

[2] Alfred Kazin, in his foreword to Sidra Dekoven Ezrahi, *By Words Alone* (Chicago: The University of Chicago Press, 1980), xi.

[3] The Holocaust, whilst clearly a species of genocide, was applied in the first instance to the mass killing of the Jews. The term, with its religious connotations of sacrifice, was generally considered repugnant by the Jews themselves, This, in their view, was certainly not a sacrifice, but a mass slaughter. The Hebrew term 'shoah' (devastation) or the Yiddishised Hebrew 'hurban' (destruction), or the 'third destruction', placing it within the 'lachrymose' context of Jewish history. The term 'genocide' was coined in 1943, in Polish, by Raphael Lemkin to characterise the mass killings of whole nations, and particularly the Jews. See his *Axis Rule in Occupied Europe* (New York: Carnegie Institute for Peace, 1944). I am thankful to John Cooper for the Lemkin information.

[4] Ezrahi, op. cit., 3.

supposed better alternative. Otherwise, the attack has no meaning, and the satire declines into anarchy. But what happens if that alternative reality no longer exists, or has 'lost its wheels'? The nagging question posed in reference to this necessary, unavoidable, and existent body of literature, remains: is there still a refuge in the salvation of reality? For Sidra Ezrahi, literature must align itself with a position, one either of submission or of conquest.[5] Do the linkages still hold good? The revolutionary fact is that there is now in place another world, apparently obliterating traces of what has gone before. And this new world has brought about a reversed value system. The vocabulary invoked in order to verbalise this world has also changed its signification. Words which meant one thing now mean another in this unprecedented place. It has been described by David Rousset as having its own anatomy, rules and meanings. It is in short 'l'univers concentrationnaire', with its 'institution concentrationnaire'.[6] Old words took on new meanings, and were perhaps changed for ever. We now understand such apparently straightforward concepts as: Transport, Action, Selection, Mussulman (Moslem), Crematoria, Canada, in terms of the sinister Holocaust vocabulary in terms of the sinister Holocaust lexicon, and their plain, previously valid meaning slides into a subsidiary and perhaps questionable role. In such a context, literature, rational thought, the work of the imagination, all become subversive, as well as the instrument of the individual working against the persecution carried out by the brutal system. Holocaust literature then is the expression of sanity in a world gone mad, an attempt to grasp and then to present that world both to the external, imagined reader, as well as to the writer himself, engaged in the task.

---

[5] Op. cit., 7.

[6] David Rousset, *L'institution Concentrationnaire en Russie (1930-1957)* (Paris: Plon, 1959). Rousset first developed his notions of a unique 'concentrationary universe' in his earlier work, *L'univers Concentrationnaire*. (Paris: Le Pavois, 1947).

Of necessity, man is, always has been, and must remain the centre of literature's concern, however he develops, and through whatever repellent paths he makes his way. This was summed up by George Steiner thus: 'We cannot pretend that Belsen is irrelevant to the responsible life of the imagination. What man has inflicted on man in very recent time, has affected the writer's primary material – the sum and potential of human behaviour – and it presses on the brain a new darkness.'[7] Man serves as the unavoidable preoccupation of literature, even within a dehumanised frame; so the act of dehumanising, the jettisoning of the human element, itself turns into the material for consideration. Without in any way denying or sidelining the unmitigated horror of recent history, literature must still persist in its function, and, now more than ever, in the words of the memorialist and novelist of the Holocaust, Elie Wiesel (b. 1928), it still must '...create beauty out of nothingness.'[8]

What Man Can Do

Literature of the Holocaust then stands between two worlds, and serves two masters; it has to witness to what has already happened, acting as the inscribing mouthpiece of the truth. But it also has to assert the value of something other, which is both contained in itself whilst suggesting the possibility of another sphere. That sphere is not only the world which once existed, but it is the world which is always carried within. But this primary concept of truth is itself problematic. In terms of Holocaust represen-

---

[7] George Steiner, *Language and Silence* (New York: Atheneum, 1966), 123.
[8] Elie Wiesel, 'Jewish Values in the Post-Holocaust Future', *Judaism 16* (1967) 299.

tation, truth is generally understood to be authentic facticity. We are to give trust in the fact that the events represented literally happened, and on the scale, in the order, and in the manner of their appearance on the page. Many works, which in respect to form, appear to be novels, are offered up as true accounts, whether as related by first or third person narrators. This has been the source of great confusion and controversy. Works which otherwise might have been accepted as excellent and moving fictions may be judged fraudulent when considered as fact.[9] On the other hand, an account may be presented as though it were the documentary record of historical events, but is quite evidently an invented work of fiction, adopting the guise of memoir in order to convey the appearance of contemporary witness, and thus strengthen its claims to veracity. This has always been a common literary device, going back to the earliest stages of the novel, as we see for example in the case of Daniel Defoe and his *A Journal of the Plague Year*, published in 1722, but written as though a contemporaneous account in the form of a diary from the year 1665. The claim to verifiability has always been the bugbear of Holocaust literature, and has been an accepted measuring rod, both muddying the issue of literary quality, as well as the other claim to give voice to a larger truth.

This larger 'truth' may be summed up in another understanding of the word, i.e. not that this literally happened at a particular moment of time, to that specifically named individual, in precisely the manner detailed. But rather, that this is the kind of thing that happened, that it is typical, and that it can stand for a wider understanding of the event, beyond its literal facticity. This is

---

[9] See the controversies over Binjamin Wilkomirski's book, *Fragments*, which was later withdrawn by the publisher, as its claims to factual representation were refuted. For a discussion of this see Leon Yudkin, *Public Crisis and Literary Response* (Paris: Suger, 2001) 139-142, 177-182, 184-5, 192.

somewhat analogous to Aristotle's concept of the nature of poetry, as opposed to historiography, not necessarily representing the thing that actually happened, but rather the thing that could have happened: 'From what we have said it will be seen that the poet's function is to describe, not the thing that has happened, but a kind of thing that might happen, i.e. what is possible as being probable or necessary. The distinction between historian and poet is not in the one writing prose and the other verse – you might put the work of Herodotus into verse, and it would still be a species of history; it really consists in this, that the one describes the thing, and the other a kind of thing that might be.'[10] Thus, in Aristotle's terminology, poetry deals with universals, history with singulars. We may for ourselves, in the distinction that we are trying to make, translate the concept of 'poetry' as 'literature'. The literature that we are talking about is that which aims beyond the particular case. Thus, it becomes universally true, rather than just applying to the specific circumstances raised. This view though does leave us wondering why, if this be the case, so many authors do insist on the claim to fact. The answer that they would tender must lie along the lines of an assessment of historical accuracy transcending mere literary value, an assertion of the sanctity of absolute truth. For our purposes though, what we are looking for is the truth of the work, not its literal correspondence to external record, although it must also do no violence to that confirmed record, and remain true to the dominant lineaments of history. There is another kind of responsibility at work here that lies heavily on the shoulders of anyone daring to touch on those awesome events. Basically, when we have actual names, dates and events inscribed, we trust that, if there is going to be any deviation into invention of data, the bor-

---

[10] Aristotle, *On the Art of Poetry*, trans. Ingram Bywater (Ondon: Oxford University Press, 1959), 43.

derline between the two that comprises the factional outcome be clearly demarcated. We want to know what is imported into the given material, that is 'invented', not in order to proclaim its falsity, but in order to preserve the historical account. As for the fictional element, that might help to build up an even truer overall picture, and help us to understand what man is, what he has been, and of what he is capable. This exists for generations past, present, and future too.

There will always be a conundrum. The Holocaust post-dates the Renaissance, the Enlightenment, the Revolution that proclaimed equality for all, the rights of man, the subjection of dogma and doctrine to the scalpel of scepticism, the manifest progress of science and the advancement of technology, including the means and achievement of productivity. And yet all this seemed to be of no avail in the face of the reversal of the continuum in the heart of the most advanced nations of the world. How did this happen? Of course, we may never get any further in the determination of an answer. But perhaps we can learn some specifics in regard to the manner in which it happened, or, for that matter, in the way that it continues to happen. Because this, for all its horror and however we might wish to reject it, remains part of the human story. And it is a story that is of central significance to the principal victims, the Jews. Let us pile detail upon detail, not just in order to further our comprehension of why, which is itself a question that may allow of no convincing or unequivocal reply, but at least of how, if that interrogative be creatively constructed. This is the content of literature, the account of reason, deploying the tool of language and the scope of judicious imagination.

That literature in any case could not normally be the literal and factual representation of an event is a truism. Perspectives must, of their nature, change. The mere transfer from event to word on paper involves an unavoidable transformation. The word has to be selected, the time is later, the circumstances different. In the case of Holocaust writing, this is doubly true. The account could hardly have been written in the course of the event itself. There was always a time lapse, and sometimes this involved a sea change from a child's perspective to that of an adult. Years had passed, sometimes languages changed, environments exchanged, contexts transformed. Specifically, the narrative 'I' had experienced its own metamorphosis, and become something other. Of course, one could argue that all this should not affect the external circumstances described. And yet, everything involves a subjective view, and may rightfully be confirmed or challenged by another. We cannot but say that all attempted objectivity must needs be tentative, and therefore tentatively accepted in its detail.

The Point of Literature

However distasteful then, serious literature, if it wants also to be taken seriously as an intervention into the serious issues facing us, must also deal with what is most repugnant. The Holocaust was and is an outcome of human behaviour. The ambition of the writer to remain true to its actuality reached its apogee with the various expressions of documentary history, in the two dramas, *The Investigation* (1965) and *The Deputy* (1963) by the German playwrights, Peter Weiss and Rolf Hochhuth respectively, and in the novel, *Babi Yar* (1966) by Anatoli Kuznetsov. The authors' methods differ, both because the sources for documentary literature depend either on personal memory or on documented source material, and also because the premises of literary function are disparate. Weiss aspires to the presentation of raw facts, without comment, interpretation or imposed structure. Hochhuth thinks that this is not only impossible in theory – that there is no such thing as pure objectivity, that structure must be present even if it pretends not to be – but that also, such an approach would lead to moral neutrality, surely the very opposite of the objective intended. Kuznetsov takes us to the very heart of darkness, the horror of mass slaughter, allowing for no cool judgment on the part of the reader.

We must conclude that in a work of literature, not only are the active characters present, but so too is the narrative voice, whether invested in the author or in an alternative and created observer. Mankind is the subject, and it is a human who presents the record. The human being is the motor, even if the literary artifice pretends to an objectivity of observation. It is the person who observes, and by the very selection of material, of focus, of time scale, in short, of every aspect included, and that person then humanises the document in both subject and object. Some writers of course take this position to the opposite pole, and work their own tendencies and views into the text, taking in the documented material, but then working the grain of established fact in order to support a particular tendency. Clearly, if historical material is to be cited, it has to be cited honestly and authentically, otherwise it will in itself be discredited, and the very foundation of the work and of the argument therein will collapse dangerously. A Holocaust writer is not a completely free agent in the way that he would be if he were to adopt a fictional theme; he is a responsible servant to the facts as well as a creative artist. On the other hand, if literature were to refuse to engage with the Holocaust as a moment of supreme of supreme significance, and maybe as the touchstone of modern life, then he might condemn himself to marginality. It would be a strange literature indeed that did not engage with the world around, as it is, and confront its prevalent manifestations. In the twentieth century, and specifically since World War I, directed and total violence has invaded every corner of human space. The

21

act of murder and constant confrontation with premature death are no longer the exclusive province of the professional fighter, but the experience of everyman. That is why it is known as world war. And, as for the later phase, World War II and the Holocaust (the war against the Jews), this is both a sequence and a deepening of the experience, a projection of mass total hatred directed towards the extermination of a people, a genocide (a term invented to categorise this phase). Total extinction is now not only a possibility, but has been actively sought, and the means for its achievement are becoming inevitably more prevalent. Literature, as possessing the most sensitive antennae and, in language, the most cultivated instrument, as it searches out what is going on, should also be the most suitable means of record and reaction. It should help us to know and to understand, though of course that would not imply any consequent shift to soften the force of criticism and dissent.

The Reality

Sometimes it is very hard to make a viable distinction between literature and reportage. This is when the reportage becomes the literature itself, when the writing begins and ends with the conveyance of reality. This is evidently the case with the Italian writer, Primo Levi (1919-1987), whose declared intention was to record as literally, faithfully and completely as was humanly possible, in accordance with the dictates of his memory and personal experience, who was eventually to commit suicide. This is even more gruesomely so (through the circumstances that gave rise to the writing) with Tadeusz Borowski (1922-1951), the Polish writer who was also to put an end to his own life. His collection of stories, *This Way to the Gas, Ladies and Gentlemen*,[11] is almost unreadable for the unmitigated, stark horror of its contents. As Ezrahi says, this is the ultimate in 'factuality'.[12] But, as the translator says in her prefatory note: 'Despite the deceptive simplicity of his style and his documentary technique, his writing transcends the merely actual.' So, it transpires that when documentary material is conveyed with the utmost authenticity, it may constitute an art which conceals art, and create the unalloyed transmission of what happened, an external fact, i.e. factuality, but which does not retain its exclusive position on the outside, but which penetrates within too. In the stories, which are described as episodes of 'Auschwitz life', the narrator writes as 'we', as one of those present, as is the case, autobiographically. He is in an ambiguous position, obviously a victim, but also playing the part of one of the perpetrators, a forced collaborator on the scene. His function is to clear the corpses, and thus, living off the prisoners, surviving then through the transports, removing goods from the victims, on the verge of extermination. The 'Canada' teams to which the narrator is assigned shove these human remains upstairs. We have descriptions of crazed crowds, blind terror, threshing around, panic, and, the worst horror of all, crushed infants, seen as repulsive vermin. But there is still time for inevitable reflection, a summary of the total body count, which on the basis of a mark coin received for each victim, is estimated at around 4½ million. In the meantime, the victims hate each other, both for what is done to them and for what they are forced to do. As he says: '[I] carry out dead infants…I try to escape from the corpses, but they are everywhere.' (25) And a glance beyond yields the view of columns of smoke rising from the crematoria over

---

[11] Tadeusz Borowski, *This Way to the Gas, Ladies and Gentlemen,* trans. Barbara Vedder (New York: Viking, 1967) (first pub. 1959 posthumously).
[12] Ezrahi, op. cit., 50-61.

Birkenau. We, the readers, are both here, in Auschwitz, and beyond, accompanying the tortured author in an overall reckoning. And we ask, 'why? Why should we do this?' The answer must surely lie somewhere in the need to enter the common terrain of human beings and human action, in its actuality. It is hugely painful to imagine it, and then to confront it; but it must be done. The ultimate is reached. In another story, 'A Day at Harmenz', each individual victim jokes about what is to happen when the other's turn comes up to go to the gas. A Jew, Becker, defends himself against the charge of cruelty when he had been a 'camp senior', by explaining what is meant by real hunger: ' "Real hunger is when one man regards another as something to eat." ' (34) The inmates sing a popular song called 'Cremo'. And that day, they are expecting another Selection, a fact which means that it will be the end for most of them, especially for those weakened by trial and exhaustion. In another story, 'The People who Walked On', the narrator, clearly at this stage a privileged inmate, is playing football outside, in a good position to observe the camp as a whole. He notices an enormous transport being herded in. But he is concentrating on the game, takes his eyes away for a moment or two, and when he looks up again, they are all gone, no sign of them: ' "Between two throw-ins in a soccer game, right behind my back, three thousand people had been put to death." ' (64) These are the mass killings. But the narrator retains more the individual flashes, and he records: 'Your memory retains only images.' (77) This writer is witness, victim, forced collaborator, inscriber at the heart of the killing. In the story, 'Auschwitz, Our Home (A Letter)', there is a cool description of the casual killing of 2-3 million with such determined dispatch that no one else really knows about it. He puts the question of why there seems to be no perceptible protest: 'What is this mystery? This strange power of one man over another? This insane passivity that cannot be overcome?' (92-3) He persists in his aspiration, the ardent desire of the letter writer addressing the unknown and probably non existent recipient: 'I do not know whether we shall survive, but I like to think that one day we shall have the courage to tell the world the whole truth and call it by its proper name.' (102)

We see from this that Borowski is not merely presenting an account of the bare facts, necessary as this primary function is. He is also appealing to the readership and to the world beyond. The genre of the literary letter of course transcends its immediate and apparent function, addressing the totality of possible and potential readers, present and future. In this case, Borowski is carrying out the task called for in that letter, calling to all to listen to his witness. And it is a task shared by all Holocaust writers, making them a very special, suffering but privileged breed.

There is another class of Holocaust writers, escapees, those who bore close witness, but managed to get out. Their testimony is intimate and invaluable, painful, as it is accompanied by an awareness of how close they came to annihilation. Such is the Viennese born Jakov Lind (b. 1927), who continued to write in German, after he had escaped to and lived successively in Holland, Israel and England. His most notable and angry story is 'Soul of Wood',[13] a third person account of a transport from Vienna to Auschwitz, which the central character, Anton Barth, managed to avoid. It opens with the chilling sentences: 'Those who had no papers entitling them to live lined up to die. The whole North-west Station was a gigantic waiting-room.' Anton lives with the consciousness of the proximity of death, and the chance escape. But it is only an escape from physical and immediate extermination, not from the mental torture. As he says: 'I was born in a bloodbath, a deluge of

---

[13] The title story in Jakov Lind, *Soul of Wood*, trans. from German Ralph Manheim (London: Jonathan Cape, 1964); orig. pub. as *Eine Seele aus Holz* (Berlin, 1962).

blood. But I didn't drown in it. Maybe that's where my sickness came from?' (9) From there on, the narrative becomes surrealistic. Anton is a paralytic, entrusted to the care of a war invalid, Hermann Wohlbrecht, who enlists the aid of his epileptic brother-in-law, Alois to save Anton. The story winds its crazy way to the end of the war, when they come for Anton, and Wohlbrecht is killed. But the surrealistic form of the story does not lessen its autobiographical implications, and has to be deconstructed. Lind himself writes, in his explicitly autobiographical essay, 'Jahrgang 1927' (1967): 'The totally crippled Anton Barth, who becomes a roe in his forest hiding place ... is me.'

Another late and retrospective view of the events, as presented by a victim, is the work of the Polish language writer, Ida Fink (b. 1921). Her own life is one of hiding in order to escape and survive. She was born in the town of Zbaraz, Galicia (now the Ukraine), went underground during the occupation, and emigrated to Israel in 1957. Her exquisite collection of stories, *A Scrap of Time*,[14] constitutes a multi-faceted, late recollection of the occupation and its effects. These were so devastating that, as she shows, time itself came to be measured differently. The tone is elegiac, measured and considered, the writing economical. It is a response delayed by forty years. But for all the restrained quality of the prose, the searing nature of the mass atrocities is not lessened. Sometimes, the account of such is presented by another character in the stories, as for example, by the household assistant, Agafia. All phases of the killing operations are noted; different points of time, as fitting in with the various phases of the murderous program, and presented by different people, compose an overall picture of the extermination of the individuals, families, and the

---

[14] Ida Fink, *A Scrap of Time*, trans. from Polish Madeline Levine and Francine Prose (New York: Schocken Modern Classics, 1987). This volume was published in Polish in the course of the same year, in England.

totality of the population. Thus, not only the Holocaust, but its permanent effect, are most powerfully conveyed.

Death in the Holocaust differs from the normal death accompanied by the rites and ceremonies attendant. Certainly it is not in accordance with the heroic death accompanied by public burial and memorial. Here, there is no family, and, as it appears to the victims, apparently not even any survivors to regret the passing, of the deceased, or even to note the fact of death. All that envelops the scene is desolation, and the body sinks disgraced anonymously, as nothing more than waste, no preexistent life, no spirit or soul, just physical residue. If the Nazi programme is carried out, as seemed only too probable to the victims, there will be a total vacuum left behind. The family will be gone, and the enveloping society, the race, the civilisation will have disappeared. There is no support system. All that remains is a meaningless hole.[15] The dying have their supplications, sustained by the memory of others. It is this unfulfilled function gone unheard, and its implicit request, that Holocaust literature seeks to express. It is this yawning gap that it fills.

We have seen here alternative ways into the writing up of the direct experience. The stark representation in all its horror in the ultra realism of Borowski takes us to the edge of that possibility. Lind opens naturalistically, but then moves off the surface into a surreal mode, thought here to be more appropriate to the events set out. And Ida Fink contrasts the two worlds, that of her childhood with that of the Nazi occupation. These are so utterly different in kind that they must be marked out by the two ways of measuring time. We have moved into a new epoch, and everything will now be measured according to another scale. One factor making for a radical shift of target is precisely the lack of the previously

---

[15] This point is discussed in Ezrahi, op. cit., 62-68.

existing community. Once, there had been a corporate entity, albeit an entity of sufferers, sharing a common fate, history, and, maybe, of expectation. Now, there is an empty space, and the writer does not know the addressee, nor even, whether there is such. The uncertainty of the target is matched by the tentative nature of the address. The community of Yiddishists, for example, has virtually disappeared. The Hebrew community too has shrunk, and is now confined to a single space on the map. The function of language is now not so much to communicate within a shared catchment, as to make some sort of statement, and to point to itself in the twilight.

Points of View

Holocaust literature can be divided into various categories, depending on the point of view adopted in the writing. There is the writing from the stance derived from the experience of the death camp itself, from within the cauldron. There is the story of the person hidden, perhaps under an assumed identity, or, for all intents and purposes, invisible. There is the experience of the person on the margins, both outside and within, and sometimes moving from one sphere to another. Then, there is the tale of the total outsider, beyond the arena where the action is taking place. Then there is the reconstructed perspective from the following generations take their position, effecting that reconstruction, either in event or in judgment. Whether through memory, observation, imagination or analysis, the writing can be a legitimate way into the key event of the last century.

Because of the startling nature of the deviation from behavioural norms manifest in the Holocaust, literary reaction has to struggle to find appropriate tools of representation and reaction.

These should be both adequate to the subject matter in both accuracy and gravity. Some writers might think that to continue their work along the trusted and traditional lines would suggest that nothing particularly radical has occurred to effect a breach with the past. Literature, and in particular the novel, the creation of the new and the mirror of the contemporary world, has always reflected the reality that has contained it. So a world which has brought about the Holocaust has dug a hole into previously held assumptions. The act of creative writing needs to represent that too, not just through its content but also in the manner of address. So it is that the breaking of the chain and disjunctive responses are so characteristic of Holocaust writing. Apart from anything else, it will give us pause, slow down our reading, check the sequences, and rethink our assumptions. The French novelist, Georges Perec (1936-1982), in his literary games, suggests a world beyond the text, but also through the text itself. The novel, *La Disparition* (1969) is not only called 'Disappearance' (also 'death'), but is also about death. Amazingly, the letter 'e' is omitted throughout the course of the whole book, and 'e' is, as we know, the most commonly used letter in an average French text (and in an average English text too, for that matter). But, beyond that, it transmits a further omission, because, in French, the letter 'e' is pronounced identically with the word 'eux', meaning 'them'. What is missing in Perec's autobiography is precisely 'them', those others who were cut down, and were thus missing from Perec's life. The author's own life story is about a gap, and is a gap in itself. This literary game is not just a tour de force, but the analogical representation of the story told. The Israeli writer, Yoel Hoffman (b. 1937), has built up his stories of immigrants from Europe to Israel by both entering their thinking world and consciousness, and slipping blanks pages following every page of text. Not all thoughts, it may be suggested, can be reproduced in adequate verbal language. The silences should be there too, and thus the blanks give not only an optional space, but force the reader into a pause, in which he himself is a participant in the creation of the total form. Both of these writers are searching out ways of expression, not just for the sake of innovation, but in order to match the means to the end. In the stories and novels of the German language writer, who lived in England, W. G. Sebald (1944-2001), integrated photographs into his text, attempting to extend the range of setting out the actuality of the interrupted lives of the 'emigrants', who were not allowed to continue their own life story according to the normally accepted and expected sequence. So things were forgotten, repressed, and bubbled up only later as the recreation of a censored and painful past, as though from another planet. The works by these authors all seek new tools to recreate a disrupted world.

And the writers of the next generation, affected and in fact themselves formed by the experience of the previous, face their own world and the need to find means of appropriate narration for their situation. Although historically, it might well take place beyond the parameters of the Holocaust span, it is by no means free of it. On the contrary, it is to a large extent derived from it. Hence the need, in the second generation and beyond, again to find a suitable form for the new life of the post-Holocaust person. The Israeli short story writer and novelist, Savyon Liebrecht (b. 1945), in her transparent and traditionally related stories of Israeli life, brings the residue of the Holocaust into the focus of the younger generation, whether that generation wills it or not. The overflow is there, and forms an essential element of life beyond. How is this new story to be told? The writing searches out possibilities. And the same is true for writers who did not themselves go through the experience, neither directly, in their own lives, and nor in the lives of their parents, who were not survivors in the strict sense of the term. A need is felt here to imagine the situation as forcefully, as truly, and as freshly as possible, as we see in the work of the younger Israeli novelist, David Grossman (b. 1954). In order to see afresh what has become a cliché, he sets before us a nine-year-old child in the first section of *See Under: Love* (1986), a section which then shapes the rest of the novel. For the child, everything to do with the experience, is of its nature new, and thus free of previously held assumptions. This is another way into the retelling. The whole exercise of retelling, recreation, the search for new forms, is the search for an appropriate framework, to make us see again, and the writer tell again, in different ways. This is part of the story, and the storyteller cannot just repeat the method and telling, as had been carried out before. There would be no point. Particularly so when we have to deal with a world so fundamentally changed.

Despite the formidable obstacles placed in the way of immediate reportage on the actuality of the events, good, reliable and full accounts from the very heart of the furnace have survived. These do preserve the maximum of authenticity and reliability, as they represent the contemporary situation, in all its changes and ferocity, not recovered in retrospect, but bearing the sense of the time of its making. There are three diaries, part taking the form of memoirs, written in conditions of privation and danger, originally inscribed in Yiddish or Hebrew, but more easily now available in English.[16] But apart from such contemporaneous accounts, there is still something special about Holocaust literature, about its urgency and intensity, about its need for transmission, and its emergence from the most dreadful and extensive historical episode

---

[16] See the following: Emmanuel Ringelbaum, *Notes from the Warsaw Ghetto*, trans. Jacob Sloan (London: McGraw-Hill Book Company, 1958). Based on the selection printed in *Bleter far geszichte* (Warsaw, 1948). Chaim Kaplan, *Scroll of Agony*, trans. from Hebrew and ed. Abraham Katsh (New York: Macmillan, 1965). Michael Zylberberg, *A Warsaw Diary, 1939-1945* (London: Vallentine, Mitchell, 1969).

imaginable. As Alvin Rosenfeld has written: 'An age is known not only by the books it produces but by those it labors to preserve and pass on to succeeding generations. On both counts - that of original creation as well as that of vital cultural transmission – Holocaust literature must be counted among the most compelling literatures of our day.'[17] Rosenfeld calls his own book, 'A Double Dying', as, deriving from Wiesel's characterisation, not only did man die, but also the idea of man.[18] In all, the literature of the Holocaust must be the central narrative point for contemporary Jewry in particular, as it is Jewry against which this was primarily directed, and carried out with such spectacular results. But it can also be seen as the marker for a new point in the history of the modern world overall, and thus poses a test for the writer in that context. In this light, we see that the Holocaust is not situated exclusively in the past, covering the dates of its operation, but, with its antecedents and after effects, hovers potently over all successive generations, everywhere. We may note too that much literature in general that postdates the Holocaust, even when the action therein is specifically placed in an earlier era, bears the marks of Holocaust consciousness. This is particularly so in 'Jewish literature', that is, in the literature dealing with Jewish characters and illuminating the Jewish situation. Examples of such are the novels of Bernard Malamud, *The Fixer*, or I. B. Singer's *The Slave*, the former set in pre-revolutionary Kiev, and the latter in seventeenth century Poland.[19] The literature of the Holocaust, explicit or implicit, rather than subsiding or fading out, is constantly renewed, and the challenge posed by the subject to find adequate expression, remains. For

---

[17] Alvin H. Rosenberg, *A Double Dying: Reflections on Holocaust Literature* (Bloomington: Indiana University Press, 1980), 4.

[18] Elie Wiesel, *Legends of our Time*, trans. Steven Donadio (New York: Holt, Reinhart and Winston, 1968), 190.

[19] See Rosenfeld, op. cit., 67.

those inside the event, there is the question of 'why literature?' in the face of such a dreadful fact. It can never be truly its analogue. For those contemporaries outside, there is the need for confrontation and appropriation, to take over its internality. For successor generations, there is the need for historical imagination in the unravelling of a deep puzzle, which still asserts the capacities of human kind. The tool is the word, and the word itself may be transcended to become the material articulated. But all literature does inevitably engage with that material, the phenomenon of the Holocaust, and then it seeks to find some suitable garb in order to render the apparition visible, if not graspable.

It is possible that the reader may be so overwhelmed by the enormity of the subject that all critical response is dulled. James Young has written: 'Unfortunately, the sheer horror at the core of the Holocaust has often swamped other, more important historical and literary questions.'[20] There are separate issues involved here, such as the events themselves, and the nature of their representation, although Young goes on to say that his approach '[r]ecognizes that literary and historical truths of the Holocaust may not be entirely separable.'[21] Even what is seen and reported by the participants themselves may in return be the product of external manipulation. It is difficult to distinguish truth from falsehood with any degree of absolute validity, as they may merge into each other. What one person records must be absorbed into another scale of events, within which that takes place. We may wish to assign greater credence to personal experience and memory than to the *post factum* sifting of evidence, but this latter may be in a better position to take account of other relevant facts, beyond the

---

[20] James Young, *Writing and Rewriting the Holocaust; Narrative and the Consequences of Interpretation* (Bloomington: Indiana University Press, 1988), vii.
[21] Ibid., 1.

ken of the former. This is not so much a distinction between subjective and objective, as between limited perspectives, which can then be enlarged to take others into account. But then this larger view itself, although more inclusive, will not be in receipt of the claim to the authenticity of the primal experience. This internal dialectic goes on; the fact and its narrative. In sum, the narrative becomes part of the larger and more inclusive fact. As Rosenfeld argues, the expression of the material takes place against the awareness of the limitations of language, and tends towards silence. But it has no choice other than to be articulate in the best way that it knows.[22] In this lies the test for the writer, and the struggle with the raw material in the making of the literature. This raw material is the experience as recorded by the eye, by word of mouth, and by language. But it is then transmitted in language, the language of all the various strands of oral and written residue, and it is not necessarily pliable. The sources for the use of language may be personal memory, documented material from first hand sources, or the creative use of the imagination. One is not necessarily a more valid base than another. It is the final result that makes its decisive claim on our judgment. The writer accesses all the above in the ambition to remake the model, as there is no point in just repeating what is already there. There is no other viable option than to use it in by any means available. The reader must then contend with such issues as differentiation and preference in response.

---

[22] See Rosenfeld, op. cit., 86-95.

II

THE STATUS OF KA-TZETNIK

Background

'Ka-Tzetnik 135633' (Yehiel Dinur, 16 May 1909-17 July 2001) was one of the first to write from the furnace of Auschwitz, chronicling its horrors in detail, pressing himself into the service of accurate memorial as a novelist narrator.[1] Born Yehiel Feiner, he is known as Ka-Tzetnik 135633 (a Polish word, meaning a member of a concentration camp, followed by the prisoner number, which was issued by the camp authorities, and based on time of entry), having renamed himself with his concentration camp number tattooed on the skin of his arm. He was born in Sosnowiec, Poland, presumably the town behind the fictional name of Metropoli in his writings, son of Abram Fajner and Idessa Skornik, members of a Hasidic family, and grew up in his grandfather's farm. He received a traditional and intensive Jewish education, studying (as he claimed, although this claim has been disputed by his acquaintances, who say that there is no supporting evidence of it) at the famous Talmudic academy, called 'yeshivat hakhmey lublin'. It is

---

[1] See list of Ka-Tzetnik's books and translations in bibliography.

presumably Sosnowiec that is the town behind the fictional name of Metropoli that appears throughout his writings as the home setting of Harry, the chief protagonist and reflective consciousness in his work. He very early started to write music and poetry in Yiddish, also becoming well known in orthodox circles as a polemicist, arguing for the creation and acceptance of an orthodox literature, rather than abandoning the field to the secularists. But, following his experiences at Auschwitz, where he was imprisoned during the war for two years from 1943 until the liberation, he made every effort to consign his early work to oblivion. After wandering in Europe, he was hospitalised in Italy by members of the 'Jewish Brigade'. After his marriage, he hebraised his name to Yehiel Dinur (literally meaning 'out of the fire'), but insisted on being known as KT 135633, adopting his concentration camp number, in 1943, as his name. He assumed the name Karl Tsetniki during 'Brikha' (flight from Europe) and immigration to Mandatory Palestine.[2] He reconstituted his identity, even changing the date of his birth for public consumption, (he is generally described as having been born in 1917), not out of free choice, but through the dreadful circumstances that were forced on him.[3] His whole identity is now to be subsumed by these awesome experiences. They were so traumatic that he felt impelled not only to renounce

---

[2] An interesting article, dealing with the issue of the author's pseudonymous presentation is Jeremy D. Popkin, 'Ka-Tzetnik 135633: The Survivor as Pseudonym', *New Literary History*, vol.33.2, The University of Virginia. (2002), 343-355, where the author's objective is described as depersonalisation. The function of the adoption of this 'anonymous pseudonym' is that '[i]t frees readers to confront what he presents as the one and only aspect of who he is.'

[3] An additional byproduct of the adoption of the surname, according to Popkin, is the author's detachment from aesthetic concerns. Thus, 'Ka-Tzetnik' is not seen as a pseudonym, but as his real identity. The lack of psychological depth noted by the author's critics, including those who exclude him from the canon of serious Holocaust writers, may also derive from this stripping of individual identity from the victim.

his pre-Auschwitz work, but to accept the dehumanising mark of the concentration camp label, which consisted of a number in place of a name. From that point onwards, his decision was to subsume his individual identity within the larger collective association of the victims. It may be this too, which has led him to describe the experiences of the victim do openly and frankly, and to reject any pre-Auschwitz stratum as a significant subject for his writing. On at least three occasions, he burned the book of poetry under the name Yekhiel Fajner. He also made a new start to his literary work, and declared that he would take neither individual credit nor financial benefit from it. He sought in this way to be submerged into a collectivity, that of the concentration camp inmates. He wrote his works in both Yiddish and Hebrew. For him, Hebrew was the holy tongue (*leshon ha-qodesh*), and Yiddish the language of the martyrs (*leshon ha-qdoshim*). It was not until the Eichmann trial in Jerusalem of 1961that it became generally known who the signatory Ka-Tzetnik was in historical reality, and what were his original and adopted names.

Almost immediately after the war, he went to Palestine/Israel, and he entitled his early classic novel, *Salamandra*. A salamander, according to legend, is a reptile that can live in fire, a further use of the fire image in the characterisation of his work. According to the ancient Hebrew sources, a 'salamandra' [*sic*] is a reptile of fire, and whoever soaks himself in the blood of the salamandra becomes fireproof (see Babylonian Talmud, *Hagigah* 27a, where a parallel is drawn between the *talmid hakham*, the scholar, and the salamandra). So he seems to see himself now as made of fire, like the traditional scholar, and thus he was inevitably impervious to any further fire damage. He wrote the work in Italy in Yiddish (that original version no longer extant) in the immediate aftermath of the liberation. It was first published in a Hebrew translation by Y .L. Barukh in 1946 (later issued in an English translation by his wife Nina under the title of *Sunrise over Hell* in 1977). He published the book under a pseudonym amounting to anonymity, only with his concentration camp number, as he thought of himself as writing in the name of the otherwise anonymous dead. Like so many other Holocaust writers, he disclaimed any literary nature in the work. In his evidence at the Eichmann trial, held in Jerusalem in 1961, he said: 'This [Ka-Tzetnik] is not a literary name. I do not see myself as a writer of 'literature'. This [*Salamandra*] is a chronicle from the planet Auschwitz, whose inhabitants had no names. They were not born, and did not give birth, did not live and did not die. They breathed according to other natural laws, where every split second moved on the wheels of another time. Their names: Ka-Ttzetnik, the skeleton of a number.' This was the first time that he emerged from anonymity. He is the Auschwitz writer par excellence, chronicling the horrors of that place in literal detail. He was one of the first to emerge and to write from the furnace, a rare survivor, but also a storyteller, pressing himself into the service of accurate memorial. He lived for his writing, and the writing in the post-Auschwitz world is the penning of the record. To such a degree did he experience the transformation that he disclaimed all his pre-Auschwitz writing, going as far as to destroy the single copy of his early Yiddish poetry in the National Library of Jerusalem in 1991, an interesting take on Adorno's famous dictum on the impossibility of writing poetry after Auschwitz. In this case, as Omer Bartov points out, it is the writing of poetry before Auschwitz that is illegitimate, as the world must subsequently adopt a new stance in the light of the events that had taken place. The end of his life indeed is marked by a return to the conditions of Auschwitz. Antony Rudolf says in his obituary, metaphorising his mental return to the primary experience: 'When he died, he weighed 30 kilos. In mind and body [*sic*], he had returned to Auschwitz.'

His Palestine/Israel period creatively opens in 1947, when he married Nina Asherman, a writer, already settled in Palestine. She had read *Salamandra,* and then became one of his translators. He published the book again in 1971, this time in his own Hebrew version, together with a new novel, *Ha-imut (The Confrontation).* There are clear links in imagery and metaphorisation between this, his first novel, and his first literary efforts. One such link is the role that he ascribes to the function of the Jewish writer, which he early compared to the people's representative in the synagogue who leads the prayers (*sheliah tzibur*). But, in the later editions of *Salamandra,* this notion is omitted. There are indeed substantial differences between the published versions, as well as between them and the Yiddish manuscripts as reconstructed through Hebrew translation.

His Biography

To produce a reliable account of Ka-Tzetnik, the man and the writer, is problematic. Although a contemporary, he has covered his traces with multiple identities. He has changed his name twice. His date of birth has been given wrongly as 1917, eight years out, according to most reliable estimates. His actual birth date is hinted at in his first publication, the Yiddish collection of poems in Yiddish in 1931, titled *Tsveyuntsvantsik* (i.e. 'Twenty-two', alluding to his own age, and thus disclosing his date of birth as 1909). But however much the traces have been physically obliterated, (literally, after the physical destruction of the book in 1991, the images over that period remain consistent. In the preface to the Yiddish collection, he compares the function of the poet '[t]o a people's representative on the holy mountain of poetry. He is the eternal image of his environment. He is the fiery (again fire - LY) arrow making actual the potential, spiritual energies within the tribe or people.' This image comes up again in *Salamandra* in the speech of one of the fighters who sees the military arm as pioneers heading the camp, who will be followed by the others. But he has attempted, by implication, and, as we noted, later explicitly, to obliterate all traces of his pre-Auschwitz writing career. He is a bilingual author, in Yiddish and Hebrew, often writing the work in both languages, and it is sometimes unclear which version is primary. And then, to add to the bibliographical complications, many versions of his books have appeared under separate imprints, where sometimes whole sections have been extracted for separate publications (for example, for the Israeli army series, *Sifriyat tarmil*), extracted without attribution, and also, on the other hand, there are occasions when later prints have combined separate original publications. In English translation, following the Hebrew originals, the Holocaust existence recreated has been rendered in a quintet of novels, with the titles: *Sunrise over Hell*, *House of Dolls*, *Star Eternal*, *They Called him Piepel*, and *Phoenix over the Galilee*. *House of Dolls* has been translated into over twenty languages, and has sold over five million copies. Presumably because of the enormous commercial success of the work and its lurid subject matter, the exploitation of Jewish girls for sexual purposes, the author has been charged with the creation of pornography and kitsch. But Ka-Tzetnik rewrote the book five times in order to try to expunge any traces of commercial overwriting, and he regards his work as an act of faith in humanity. *House of Dolls* tells the story of Daniella Preleshnik, sister of Harry, who is the chief character and focus of narrative consciousness throughout the author's opus. This quintet of novels, or novel in five parts, is that part of the author's opus which sets out the narrative of Auschwitz, the chronological and family background, the sequence, and the concentration camp setting itself. The later works attempt to arrive at a consideration of the meaning of the events and the implications for contemporary and future life.

Generic definition of the author's opus is difficult, because, although the structure of each work is fictional, including the invention of many of the place names and characters, he is very careful to remain faithful to the historical narrative and sequence. So there is a mixture of documentary chronicle and fictional framework of which the reader has to be aware. Clearly, all that pertains to psychological projection, speculation, description of mental states and suchlike, is, of necessity, within the realm of fiction. Many incidents are repeated. It is a characteristic of Ka-Tzetnik's narrative technique to reprise events already recorded in another section of the sequence and to relate them somewhat differently.

The Shaping of Biography

The chronicle overall takes us throughout the author's life, presenting an account of Harry Preleshnik's life, his background with his sister, Daniella, and their early dreams of emigration to the Land of Israel. In many respects, this fictional account is paralleled by the events of his actual biography. Although he had been massively savaged by his life experience, he sought to contribute to the current betterment of his fellow humans, and specifically, to the improvement of Israeli society. He was, for example, active in a society for the encouragement of Arab-Israeli relations, and together with his wife, he formed the Israeli Movement for Arab-Jewish Cooperation in 1965. He saw this concern as stemming from the nature of his life and experiences. In fact, his total literary output is a translation of his life into a chronicle of several parts in the form of novels. These are not works of fiction, but rather a transparent writing up of his own experiences, as well as those of the people close to him.

His story, as recorded in *Salamandra* (in 1971 republished together with its sequel, *Ha-imut*) takes up the account of Harry, from his youth, when he was still, in the terminology of the author, an individual, right through the German occupation. But he then includes his incarceration and death camp experiences. It is a third person account, and, although it seems to follow the contours of his own biography fairly closely, it sets up fictional names of characters and places. Thus, it constitutes a form of faction. In a sense, it is the most important novel in the overall chronicle, as it serves as the template for the rest. Here we see that *Salamandra* also gives its name to the work as a whole. The novel constitutes the backbone of the author's opus, setting the scene, defining the characters and the situation, and creating the historical background, well known about the Poland at the early stages of the Nazi invasion. The chronicle seeks to demonstrate the movement from the state of individuality to the obliteration of that identity. According to the motto at the head of the work, although all people are created according to a single image, the features of each one differ. That is the fundamental character of the human being in his/her original state. But this was decidedly not the case on that 'other planet' known as Auschwitz.

In Warsaw, in the Summer of 1939, Harry Preleshnik, the hero of the novel, as well as the focus of consciousness and most of the action, is a graduate student of the famous Conservatorium, and now a successful and popular composer. His ex-colleague and friend Leopold, an influential impresario now working in Buenos Aires, tries to persuade him to come to the American continent, where there are so many opportunities, although Harry has his heart set on Palestine, a place the thought of which fills him with elation. But his beloved betrothed Sonia and her father are opposed to the notion of emigration. Although Solomon Schmidt, the father, had himself emigrated to Palestine, he nevertheless advises 'caution' to his daughter, thus influencing her to stay put in Poland. So romance is mixed in with a dire political situation, apprehended with good cause, but disastrously underestimated. But even he, Schmidt, successful industrialist that he was, had begun to think that he had no place in Poland and that it was not his land. So he was always to be a foreigner there, and he had decided to emigrate. Harry himself had always been convinced that his place was in Palestine, but now, at the crunch moment in the late Summer months of 1939, he had made a fateful decision not to obey his own instinct and leave Poland. Then, on September 1, Hitler invaded Poland in order to bring it under his control. Many of the Jews had contrived a sophisticated urban environment in their Polish homeland, in which they had been both native and estranged. On the one hand, they had acted as true Europeans, and, on the other, Harry's hosts, the Safrans, had taken the trouble to speak Hebrew in their house. In the streets, meanwhile, violent anti-Semitism was on the increase, threatening all. The German war cries were welcomed by many of the Polish soldiers, who saw the Nazis as their allies in the clearing up of Jewish vermin. And, as for the Jewish population of Poland, when the attack came in the form of a Blitzkrieg, it was so sudden and absolute that there was no possibility of escape by crossing the border. The country was sealed up overnight, and it was open season on the Jews. The transition from normality to terror is not only grasped in its speed, but in scrupulous attention to detail. Horror descends from the outside, and is confirmed within; the enemy is everywhere, both in German and in Polish form, although one is the attacker and the other is apparently at home. We see that crisis, the situation of extremes, brings out both the bad and the good in people. The historical experience of war, specifically World War I, had allowed trade, and those who knew how, had learned to prosper. There is terror, and then famine. The place of the despised *Judenrat* (Jewish Council) as a pawn of the Nazis is presented from all sides, together with the awesome choices with which the members were faced. Harry himself makes the heroic sacrifice, and refuses his friend Leopold's offer to bring him to Buenos Aires, where he would be able to receive Argentinean citizenship. He is unwilling to leave Sonia, now his wife, even to save his own life, just as he is also unwilling to countenance any cooperation with the *Judenrat*, something which he would regard as collaboration. Until the actual point of exile, we witness the increasingly cruel restrictions, the public executions, and the expulsions. The point of exile, first whispered and then spoken, is Auschwitz, a name whose significance was not appreciated at the early stages, and is seen as a destination of mystery. But until his own exile, Harry, like Sonia, has to work, in dreadful conditions, in a factory. Even that though can be seen as a sort of relief in the light of what was to follow. The transports were to increase, and the word 'judenrein' was heard repeatedly, so the effort to clear the Jews out was in the process of implementation. The personal accounts of Harry, Sonia and Daniella are emblematic of the larger history, that of the destruction of the Jewish people. The process is cruel, and seemingly inevitable. But there are still options, and the tale is of one of those options narrowing, although the protagonists still struggle in making their choices. Harry and Sonia differ as to how they should act, the former for flight from the ghetto despite all the dangers, and the latter for working within the familiar environment for all its horror, in the hope that salvation might suddenly come. The process might after all go into reverse, as it has done before, she thinks. However, as the reader knows with hindsight, this did not happen here, and the catastrophe turns virtually absolute. There are scenes of horror as the bunkers, in which various families had improvised a hiding place, are destroyed and those within captured are killed. The remnants are transported to the 'other planet', his characterisation of Auschwitz, a term that becomes familiar in the Ka-Tzetnik opus.

On this planet, it seems that there are Jews as well who operate the system, Yiddish speakers amongst those in charge, picking off treasures, issuing orders, and extracting valuables. Here it is that people, that is to say, individuals identified by names, are turned into numbers, which are tattooed on the left arm. And an important lesson is learnt; anyone who wants to live has to kill. Each has a number, and they all have the common soubriquet, 'katzetnik'. Here they are in Birkenau, the killing fields of Auschwitz, the venue of the crematoria, the gas chambers, and the torture cells. The book follows the lives of the main protagonists in parallel. Harry faces the tortures of hell, but he constantly bears Sonia's command in his mind. This is the command to live. The border of losing that fundamental impulse constantly awaits with increasing force. It takes him to the edge of being a 'Mussulman' (camp slang for one who has lost the will to live). Such a 'Mussulman' has no feelings, not even hunger, although he still clings to his portion of bread as a memory of what once held him. He cannot retain food, and first he dies spiritually, then physically. Harry struggles against sinking into this, and then miraculously saves himself by getting into a coal box. When he appears later, a German officer allows him to work in a department for checking out the corpses, and so he recovers from this penultimate state. Then Sonia's story is followed up from the assembly point in town, which she refuses to attend, no longer constrained by the need to stay alive for her now absent lover. She manages to join up with a group of partisans with whom she carries out an effective series of attacks. Then she receives a permit to Switzerland, but the carriage of the train on which they travel is redirected by the Gestapo, and taken to

Auschwitz. There, convinced of the final end of Harry, she becomes a 'Mussulman', and is sent to the crematoria. At the liberation by the Red Army, Harry finds himself almost a 'Mussulman', as he joins the corpses and awaits the tanks. He is determined to abandon the graveyard, which is Poland, for good and all. But, in the second part of the novel *The Confrontation*, really a separate work, he returns to the ghetto to try to feel what freedom is really like. All he does feel however is that he has committed the great sin, and this is substantiated by the fact that he continues to live. The natural reaction should be the impulse to revenge, he asserts. But he has difficulty in finding that sense. The Red Army is exulting in victory, but he can only feel estranged and alienated, belonging to no one. In fact, he seems to be a corpse, like all those lying around: 'He felt no joy in the victory, and none at revenge'. (18). There is just a hopeless search for adequate response. The principal setting of the *The Confrontation* is Tel Aviv. The Jewish State is the antithesis of what had gone before, both in its natural features; desert in place of forests, sun in place of rain, heat in place of cold. More so, there is the fundamental contrast, as he sees it, in the Jewish situation, moving towards autonomy in pace of dependence on the gentile world.

The two parts of the book attempt to link up the two parts of the Jewish experience, matching the subtitle of *Salamandra*, which is: 'Chronicle of a Jewish Family in the Twentieth Century'. The two poles are Europe, the heart of destruction, and Israel, the site of renewal. *The Confrontation* takes us with Harry from Poland, through to the South, to Italy, and then to Palestine. But before that possibility arises, the European story has to come to an end for him. For Harry there is no home any more. And this is meant quite literally. All things and all people round him have been destroyed, uprooted and exterminated. On his massive walk out of the camp, he meets up with a young girl who has obviously been

46

through similar experiences. She articulates the shared sensation, the death experience of a strange planet that no one from without will be able to share. She says to Harry: ' "No one apart from us in the whole of this world will be able to understand us. Only we two will be able to understand each other, and the our language is not the language spoken by mouth." ' (26) She goes on to say that others will never be able to enter this world, whereas the two of them would never be able to leave it. But Harry is unwilling to allow her to share his burden, and to take her with him on his journey. He gets on to a train going South, and later he is picked up by a lorry driven by one of the Jewish Palestinian group, *Brihah* (Flight). He is taken to Treviso in Italy, and then to join the meeting point in Naples, which served as a launching pad for a wave of immigration for the survivors.

Much of Harry's story, together with the sentiment arising from it, serves as a model for survivor attitudes in general, as well as for such sentiments expressed specifically in literature. When Harry arrives in Israel, he is inevitably seen as a representative of a species, that is, the species of holocaust survivor and, of course, victim. But this is just the sort of labelling that he seeks to escape. In Israel, he tells his 'host', Felix aka David, that what he wants to meet is a genuine Jewish family, healthy, wholesome, proud and integrated into the life of the community. But he feels that he is constantly being marked out for a past which is not only incredibly and excruciatingly painful, but that is shameful too. Israel should be for him not only the antithesis of the exilic experience at its most horrific, but also its negation, rather than its constant reminder.

From this point on, the book divides into two stories. The first is Harry's own, as he moves to Tel Aviv, his perception of the new Jewish city as well as its contrast with his own sense of self as a vacant space, a vacuum. The second is the story of the Israeli girl

Galilia, a volunteer in the new Jewish army of defence, the *Haganah*, soon to be the Israel Defence Force (IDF). She happens upon a book which takes her interest, and that book is the story of Harry called *Salamandra*, the first section of this novel. So the second section of the book, *The Confrontation*, constitutes a framework around a closure, and can provide a device for the author to inspect and comment on himself and his story. And we can also see a larger picture of the Jewish situation, and the way that the narrative developed into the separate arms of Europe and Israel, with the options that they suggest. As she so identifies with the Sonia of Harry's story, so she keeps saying to him in her own mind: ' "Harry, you must live." ' She particularly identifies with the last sentences of the book (which is of course the first section of the bipartite novel): 'Harry Preleshnik raised himself on his knees within the heap of corpses. It seemed that he was growing out of it.' And, of course, for her, the way that he can live is to recreate his life in the budding Jewish State. The fact that the book is of anonymous authorship can perhaps confirm the parallel invoked by the author between her handling of the book and the way that a religious woman would hold a *siddur* (Jewish prayer book). One of Ka-Tzetnik's primary themes is the insistence on the sacred project of, first, inscribing the record, which is the chronicle of what happened, and second, on its preservation and transmission. The record can be anonymous, because it does not proceed from the mind and the pen of an individual, but from one who has had individuality removed. Now, Galilia is determined to trace the author, and is prepared to change the whole further course of her life in order to pursue a different aim, in the light of what she has now learnt about the destruction of the Jews, and of the remnant that is Harry. As for Harry, his only hope is to become a person again, one that would justify the name of Phoenix, a person with an address and an account, like ordinary people around. In Palestine/Israel, he is so aware that he is being looked at as a part object, a symbol, a homeless refugee, in need of pity, even as a rival for the few homes and the small number of jobs, but not as a respected equal.

Ka-Tzetnik's Contribution to the Literature

It is from this text that we can glean much of the status of Ka-Tzetnik's specific contribution to Holocaust literature. *Salamandra* was first published in Hebrew in 1946, and was the first of its genre. It is the first work to emerge from Auschwitz, and, whether we regard it as a novel, as a memoir, or as something on the border, it is the first to tell the story of a victim from the victim's point of view. But it also brought the writer into the company of Israeli authors, albeit as an author of a separate and strange type within the existing context of the current literary scene. But his book, as well as later works which were to plough the same field, was a product of the collective, and could only emerge by luck. It was literature composed on the back of others, by a writer whose survival was purchased by luck and at their expense. So there is guilt built into the literary achievement and success. This success too was the necessary product of the record of the sensational and the horrific. This it was these that made the author, who so longed for normality, into a freak, an object of wonder rather than a companion, one of the many. But Harry has a mission, which is his purpose in life and the justification for his survival. This is not only to record his own story, which he achieved with *Salamandra*, but also to record the horrific lives of the two children for which he felt responsible, that of his sister Daniella, who was taken to the Gestapo brothel, and whose story he tells in *Bet ha-bubot* (*House of Dolls*) and of Monish the so-called

'Piepel', whose story he tells in the book of that name. But his own story has a continuation too, here in Palestine, where he now meets up with Galilia at the home of Levitan, his editor and translator. The present context is mandatory Palestine, the war of some elements with the British, and the struggle of the *yishuv* (Jewish settlement in Palestine) for an independent State for themselves and the remnants of world Jewry. Harry, a transparent mask for the author, has to weigh up and integrate three separate worlds – the world of pre-Auschwitz, the world of Auschwitz itself, and the world of post-Auschwitz. (*The Confrontation*, 100). Some of the integration can take place as Galilia starts to take the place of Sonia for Harry, and also as she sees herself as slotting into Sonia's place in his life. He immediately sees resemblances between the two women. Galilia's slogan also echoes Sonia's: ' "Harry you will live." ' And then she proposes marriage to him. So all three phases take their focus from the central theme of Auschwitz which is the theme of his overall literary output.

The narrator is omniscient throughout, although he can enter the consciousness of others in the illumination of the principal subject. He enters the mind of Galilia who is seen as the one person who really understands the meaning of Harry's writing. She is determined then to convince him that he needs her love just as he had pursued Sonia's. Despite his experiences, she sees him as not overwhelmed by negativity. If he had been, he would not have survived Auschwitz. This was made possible by sense of love, and this same sense (of course now redirected towards herself) is what can preserve him beyond. Harry recalls the death march out of Auschwitz, the shootings, and his own escape to a treetop, thus bringing the reader up to date in the plot, and, in the present, we have the news of the declaration of the Jewish State, celebrated by Harry and Galilia together in the consummation of their love. But the sequence is not of the happiest, as Galilia sees the situation in

Israel as a logical sequence of what happened in Europe. The slaughter is continuing, and eventually the *fedayeen* would murder all the Jews here too. She falls into a kind of mental illness, in which her hostility to her parents and all around seems to be rooted, in Harry's view, in her self-hatred. There are a number of features in Galilia's condition which are not fully explicated, but which rebound off her relationship with Harry. She sees the situation in Israel as to some extent a sequence to that in Auschwitz, a scene for the collective slaughter of the Jews. But she also seeks an accord between Jews and Arabs, a prominent motif of the author's later life work. The security situation is portrayed as deteriorating following the independence of the Israeli State, and this leads to a linkage between the past and present, as well as between 'there' and 'here'. She breathes in Harry's history, but she can get nothing from him orally, only a sense of the starvation through his books. It seems that she is married to a tree stump, as the top part is cut off, and she sees herself as responsible for his further misery. She has incorporated Harry's starvation by immersing herself in his books. On the other hand, Harry feels guilty that he has allowed her to translate the texts to which entry should only be allowed to those previously inoculated. But her psychological incorporation of his condition also projects her into learning for the present and into the understanding of parallel circumstances. The dread of the Jew on the part of the German and Pole can be seen in the Palestinian situation vis-à-vis Israel, but also in the Jewish view of the Arab. That is the 'confrontation', standing in for the past confrontation, and now constituting the current reality. This is the lesson that she seeks both to extract and to apply. Five years she devoted to her own Auschwitz, years of terror and deprivation, down into the depths of herself. After the last year, when she went abroad, she returned refreshed, back to her original self, and to Harry. Their work is now to be concentrated on a rapprochement between the peoples in the Land. But the current reality of hatred, hostility and murder keeps impinging, as it does at the conclusion of the book, with the blowing up of the vehicle transporting the Arab guests back to their village following a joint meeting. The contemporary projection of the lessons of Auschwitz is central to Ka-Tzetnik's thought, and it comes into his fiction.

Realism and Pornography

House of Dolls is the best known, best selling, and most excruciating of Ka-Tzetnik's works, as it concentrates on the sadistic, torture, exploitation and rape of the principal protagonist, Daniella, Harry's sister. (Incidentally, Daniella was the name that the author gave to the daughter he later bore in Israel). It is hardly a work of fiction, although it is presented in the guise of a novel. An account of the genesis of the work within the framework of *The Confrontation* has been presented, how it follows on from *Salamandra*, and is a companion volume to *Piepel*. They constitute the author's memorial to the desecration of children in Auschwitz, and they chronicle their dreadful lives, incarceration, torture and murder, written without holding back on the horrific details.

Daniella is first found working in the Nazi imposed ghetto, sorting out vast bundles of clothing which had arrived mysteriously. Objects of any value had to be surrendered to the German bosses. We then go back in time to the Summer of 1939 when she had been planning a tour at the end of August to visit the grave of the great Polish poet, Adam Mickiewicz. She is fourteen, looking after her little brother Moni, then aged seven, and adoring her older brother Harry, who is now attached to Sonia, and planning to go on *aliya* (emigration) to the Land of Israel. She wants to accompany him. A happy, normal family, whilst still aware of the

52

internal tensions in the country and uneasily wary of an impending war. There is a constantly deteriorating situation in the ghetto, but at each stage there seems to be a pause for renewed hope. Ghetto life is depicted in great detail. There is continuous life of this kind, even between 'transports', whilst awaiting final extinction. The 'actions' grow more frequent and intense, as those left behind temporarily try to work out the principles according to which these actions operate. Another echo to the approaching end here is the Aryan market for all Jewish goods. The vultures swarm from outside the ghetto over anything that might be of value. And then, to Daniella's ultimate distress, Harry is taken to a Labour Camp. Separately, Daniella is taken, together with other girls, by the Gestapo, who cynically ignore or tear up the cards which were supposed to offer them protection. This 'action' was supervised by someone from the despised *Judenrat* (Jewish Council), who comes with his list, ensuring that no one will get away. All escape routes have been closed off, no sort of cooperation has been able to moderate the total fury of the Nazi, no person, no wealth, no *proteksia*, and no card can enable anyone to flee. Now, even the ghetto looks inviting, as the terror of something worse dawns. In the meantime, Harry has been sent to the labour camp in Niederwalden. But he is later found in Auschwitz, where life is made rather easier for him, or, at least, extended, when he is appointed as a sort of 'doctor' (*sanitar*). The story moves between Harry's tale and Daniella's. It has also proved a stumbling block for those who would like to place the work and assess it, as it is an amalgam of fiction and chronicle, and it interweaves the narrative of a love, between Harry and Sonia, a deep attachment, between Harry and Daniella, and an accurate representation of the details of the Nazi camps, a faithful historical narrative. Daniella is seen from the outside, as she is moved to a *Dulag* (*Durchgangslager,* a staging camp), but also from within her own sensibilities, as she is described as feeling totally alone (152). The representation of consciousness is conducted in traditional terms, rather than through the 'stream'. But we also witness behaviour en masse of groups. The Poles, who had been such proud nationalists, are now trying to appear as *Volksdeutscher*. There are detailed descriptions of sadistic practices and horrific, random killings. But we also move to Harry's self-sacrificing behaviour, as for example when he saves a life by offering officer responsible a valuable cigarette that he had acquired. Back with Daniella we have some of the most detailed and repellent practices relayed, such as experiments on women in the 'Women's Camp', the forced prostitution in the 'Branch of Joy'. Fragments of specific incidents echo back and forth, told and re-told in different ways, also filling in episodes previously unrelated. And we have the process of Harry's process of dehumanisation, brought about by the familiarity with the camp ethos. The dénouement is somewhat improbably staged, but hugely dramatic. Harry and Daniella meet up. Harry, as a privileged inmate, finds himself in SS headquarters, in the midst of a drunken orgy where all the boundaries, those between life and death, are blurred. Suddenly there appears, amongst the other naked men and women, the lovely figure of Daniella. Only it is Daniella who calls out to him. Wandering out into the open, she is casually shot. But her notebook is saved and retained, by her friend and guardian in crisis, Fella. This is the record of Daniella's life, now set down by the author, alter ego of Harry, who is of course still alive. Harry's doctrine for his fellow inmates had been in words often repeated: ' "Don't allow yourself to become a Mussulman." ' He himself heeded this instruction from which this document, as well as the others, emerged. *House of Dolls* has been translated into over twenty languages, and has sold over five million copies. The fact that the author, as we have noted, has been charged with the writing of kitsch and pornography (Bartov) does not seem to be in place here. In fact, Ka-Tzetnik rewrote the book five times in order to expunge overwriting, and he regards the work as an act of faith in humanity.

In the novel *Piepel*, there is a parallel Auschwitz tale to *House of Dolls*. ('Piepel' is concentration camp slang for a young boy selected by heads of blocks in Auschwitz, and used for sexual purposes. The origin of the term is not known, but was in common usage.) It was particularly the weakest and the most vulnerable who were appallingly and cruelly exploited. Here we have the continuation of the author's story of Jewish life in the vicious twentieth century with the chronicle of a family (his own in disguised form). The 'piepel' is Monish, Harry's little brother, frequently referred to in the other texts. Franzel, the head of a block in Auschwitz, has received Monish as a 'present'. The piepel's duties include acting as a steward to the head of the block, as well as pleasing him in bed. But Franzel has had other piepels beforehand, and has disposed of them quite casually. So this piepel is warned by one who managed to escape Franzel's wrath before being brutally murdered that he had better look out and do all that his wits can offer to avoid the crematorium for as long as possible. It is a great pleasure for the capricious brute to act on his sadistic impulses, integrally connected to his sick sex drive. In return for this intelligence, Monish becomes a provider to Berele, the earlier piepel. That is Monish's external and horrifying world. We are also drawn into his internal world, which is naturally isolated. That world is taken up by his all prevailing loneliness and his very real orphanhood, which is not only a fact of his life, but also the abiding metaphor of his mental being. All he sees around him is the presence of death and its instruments, the electrified wires around the camp, the ghostly Mussulmen on their way to final extinction. Their presence is a constant foreshadowing of his own imminent fate. But, in the meantime, he knows that life for him depends on the immediate satisfaction of Franzel. The figure of his father, the 'pa' for whom he yearns and whom he had sought to save and await, and of whom he was now bereft, has been transformed into the nightmarish Franzel. Soon, Berele is murdered, casually and pointlessly like everyone else. New transports arrive from Theresienstadt, injecting a sense of normality with their families and healthy appearance. They write letters to friends about life in Auschwitz as though it is a holiday camp, a normal place. But that was their function and the reason that they were not exterminated immediately, just to create that illusion for a brief moment before their own disappearance. But then, back to Auschwitz reality they go on to the crematoria, and we are assured now that Auschwitz is a separate planet, distant from any other form of existence. For Monish the chief concern is that Franzel should not find another piepel. A new piepel inevitably means death to the old piepel; the two cannot be allowed to exist side by side. Death here means putting a club over the shoulders and using it as a seesaw until the body cracks. If only he could have been fat! He was constantly being told that being fat was the only way to save his skin and find favour in Franzel's eyes. Franzel liked his piepels to have some flesh on them for his gratification. Monish moves to another block and becomes piepel to a new head, Bruno. But he feels that he must escape his fate there too. For comfort he conducts a dialogue with his dead father, 'pa' or mother, 'ma', whom he hopes is still alive, as much of the action in the novel takes place within Moni's head. To be a piepel is to have a place of honour and to be safe for as long as that status pertains. But it is also very precarious, and, as with everything in Auschwitz, it is also very lonely. But what is characteristic of the inmate, before he turns into a Mussulman, is that, like any other person, he has a survival instinct. For all the torture of his abject existence, Monish would do anything to stay alive. Realising that he has lost the protection of Bruno, he would like to move to another block, this time block16, and to seek the patronage there of the head of the block, Robert, or to do anything else through which he might be saved, and he escapes immediate selection by going over to him. He is in constant dread that he would not pass selection as he is so emaciated. 'Selection' was the process by which it was decided which Jews would be gassed immediately, and which should be saved for a later date. This decision was made on the basis of fitness for labour, and those pronounced unfit were thus 'selected'. It was only the Jews who were taken in this way, notes the narrator, not the 'Poles'. Monish, after being accepted by Robert, although only for the very short term, senses that he has to get away once more the following day. He also has to escape the mass killing that is due, and so discover from where it will be taken. So apart from the horrors all around, the dreadful sights, the torture and his own unspeakable conditions, he has to have his wits about him constantly to preserve any elements of that he retains. Monish arrives at the central message of the Ka-Tzetnik opus, which is that Auschwitz is a planet separate from the rest of the world, a place where there is no concept of wife, children, family, where there is no God, nothing, not even the crematorium, just a grey stretch in which the only thing desired is a crust of bread. But to achieve that, you must use all skill available, totally selfishly. The lesson here is: if you want to live you must kill.

A detailed account of the various aspects of 'life' in Auschwitz is presented; the types of labour carried out, the hierarchy rigorously respected, the daily routine broken up by the executions and selections, the functions of the kapos, the workings of the crematoria, the struggle for survival, and then, the Mussulmänner, and the inherent risk of becoming a Mussulman, a condition in which you are totally broken physically, and completely indifferent, mentally. As for the outside, it is noted that there are no birds in Auschwitz. The atmosphere is polluted, and no free animal would live there. Even this environment allows the use of grotesque irony. The Jews have been awarded a special place in the world, a site primarily if not exclusively for them. That place is Auschwitz, a sort of promised Land (140). But, despite the fact of being a separate and wholly other planet, Auschwitz, the single setting of the book, is still subject to the passing of the times and the changing of the seasons. Despite the claustrophobic atmosphere of the book, the outside does still peep through. The war might come to an end, it is sometimes felt, even if by that time there might be no Jews left. Monish has come to the inevitable conclusion, as a veteran, that in Auschwitz one must not be good. This is a herald of the transformation of values required for contemporary living. Now, the religious protest against the actions of God, sitting on His throne, indifferent. (161) The only way to succeed here is to reverse traditional morality, to behave with the utmost callousness, and, even on the part of the Jews too, to initiate projects of cruelty and sadism. Monish is possessed by the need not to become a Mussulman, but that is precisely the process that he observes in himself. Now, he is on the final path to the crematorium, and the supervision of the commandant Höss. The ending of Monish, like the conclusion of the novel, is somewhat surreal. He escapes following a horrific beating such as always kills, and heads towards the electrified fence. Höss observes this remarkable phenomenon of the child piepel as he is swallowed up by the earth of Auschwitz.

Later Work

The fifth in the quintet of Ka-Tzetnik's exemplary novels constituting the chronicle is *Ha-shaon asher me-al la-rosh* (1960), later reissued under the new name of *Kokhav ha-efer* (1966) and translated into English as *Star Eternal* (1971). In Hebrew, it was reissued under the new title, *Ha-shaon* (1972, The Clock). It is a short, concentrated work, conveying the essence of the experience relayed in the other works in quasi poetic language, reflecting on the total, summing up, and transmitting the emotional effect of the huge loss. This is made up of the loss of community, of home, of family, of the past, as well as the loss of the sense of a basic humanity in operation. The book consists of seventeen brief chapters, including a prologue and an epilogue. The prologue sets the scene in the town of 'Metropoli', with the 'clock above your head'. The date is September 1, 1939, and the army is everywhere. But everywhere too there is anti-Semitism, and the accusation that the Jews have sold out the country to Hitler, as well as the alternative accusation that they are getting ready for war against Hitler! This is where you were born, says the narrator to himself. As this is a reflective, inclusive work, much is written in the second person, where the narrator addresses himself, attempting to draw together the threads of a life which has seen so much dramatic change and travail. So it dwells on the origins and the outcome within a very brief space, tersely written. But immediately, with the incursion of the German army, there is sudden death everywhere too. But he (you) hears a voice telling him that he must stay alive if at all possible, and so put up no foolish resistance to the brutal forces now present.

Ha-shaon is based on the other writings and the overall narrative therein, but it is more of a distillation. It is less discursive and detailed than the other works, and there is more focus on language, striving to achieve the precise characterisation of mood and accuracy, without excess. The text moves in the direction of abstraction. However, within this framework, there is abundance of details, hastily assembled – of murders, of transports. The chronology of the killing is preserved for the record. The transports began with the aged. And this seemed logical to others and to themselves, as it is natural to assume that in an ordered regime of the type set up, old people would not be profitable to the economy. What the author aspires to grasp here is the feeling experienced by the community in the grip of the atrocity. Then though, it is the turn of the children, unbelievably packed into sacks, and thrown into lorries to be taken away. The comment is: 'This is the way to the carriages.' Nothing else can be expected now. Bleaker and bleaker, Auschwitz is everywhere. To achieve maximum effect for an unprecedented situation, the prose strains for brevity. The sentences are cryptic: 'Death is your Lord.' Language is broken up, and the writing is detached from the writing self, as an object of faithful observation. Now in Auschwitz, we have literal representation, a grasp of the greyness, the blocks. But also, the pervasive feeling, only to be known by someone who had been there. The most powerful drive of all in such circumstances is hunger, the need for a food, prayer for a bowl of soup, or even the meanest crust of bread.

The new concentration on word effects is indicated in the play in tenses between present and past. The use of the present tense brings the reader in as part of the picture,[4] and the use of the past tense distances him once more, as is normal in narrative. The reader shares the narrator's sense of the experience just as he enters the skin of the collective. How strange perhaps to hang on to life so, even though that life is to be so short and painful. So does everyone, except of course the Mussulman. There is always panic

---

[4] Article by Moshe Peli, see References.

at the selections, and even in the crematoria, the victims cry out for their bread rations. At this last moment, the experience of death is made concrete, both for those who argue for its meaninglessness and for those who see it as the arena of Jacob's struggle with the angel, as does the Rabbi. But the sceptic too may be able to find some sense in the assured survival of the people outside, perhaps for those in Israel. Finally, the gates of the camp are opened, and liberation has come. At this point, in what may be seen as a kind of epilogue, the narrator expresses himself fully in the first person, and finds his vocation marked out by the experience, and the duty to fill in for the void left by the slaughter of all the others. He addresses them: 'In your ashes grasped in my arms, I swear to be your voice, for you, for the dumb and incinerated *katzet* (concentration camp inmate) I will not cease telling of you until my last breath. So help me God. Amen.' Now his existence is marked out entirely by the number on his arm. That is 'the clock above his head'. Others back in Metropoli continue as before though, with the same clock as before. Such reparations as are offered now for his losses are not only absurdly inadequate, but irrelevant in principle. The only longing that that he has is for fragments of his past, his brother, his sister, his mother, his father, and that departed community.

Much later in his literary career, Ka-Tzetnik wrote an account of the attempted cure carried out by Professor Bastians in a Leiden hospital from 8 July 1976. This is the recognition of what he thereafter called the '*katzet* syndrome', achieved through the use of the drug, LSD. Survivors are liable to duffer recurrent nightmares, taking them back to the experience o the camps. The author is constantly assailed by guilt feelings, that he is 'desecrating the look in the eyes of those who perished in the crematoria. Am I desecrating the look by taking it to Leiden?' The ultimate personal ambition of the author is to achieve normality, to be able to sleep, and to deal with the present. The experiment with LSD conducted with Bastians, as described in *Di zeung*, 1990 (Revelation), conveys an attempt to uncover the experience, details of which had been hidden from the author himself, but the significance of which was cosmic. He was concerned with the release of previously suppressed emotion to produce what is known as 'abreaction'. Ka-Tzetnik claimed that the group of letters, 'E.DM.A', served as a single code for all his Auschwitz texts. Its meaning was unknown to the author himself, but remained insistently resonant and total. In Sheintukh's investigation of the motto, the author deploys the use of charmed letters to enter the historical associations of Rabbinic martyrdom.[5] Under the effect of the drug, Ka-Tzetnik enters into a trance. But the trancelike state has a historical precedent in the sources, and he becomes, or has already become, like the prophet Ezekiel, who is described as having eaten a scroll. The narrator here too is surely possessed by a scroll, and by the necessity to record his experience. This is the only justification for his survival. As he says towards the end of his account 'Sof un onheyb': 'I am like a tree hit by lightning, covered in flames, and burning.' (137) Previously, Ka-Tzetnik had adopted the name 'Dinur' (of fire), and entitled his basic text, *Salamandra*, i.e. the reptile soaked in fire. Now, he himself is made of fire, but, like the reptile, he can accommodate himself to that fire, and can share its nature.

The Opus

Ka-Tzetnik's work, that is excluding the pre-Auschwitz material which the author sought to obliterate as belonging to another realm, can be divided into two phases. The first is descrip-

---

[5] See Sheintukh, 'A.dm.'a: leverur mafteah be-khitvey ka-tzetnik'.

tive. It sets the scene chronologically and narratologically for the road to Auschwitz, as well as being a representation of Auschwitz itself. The second phase is philosophical. It attempts to set the events in a context of meaning, and in consideration of what could be the implications for the future. Ka-Tzetnik's writing is modelled on the author's principal subject. As his soubriquet indicates, the narrator who informs the whole is tapped to the maximum of his subjectivity. The autobiographical background is barely disguised and it informs all parts of the narrative. But the author is always concerned, in his writing and in his rewriting, to ensure that objective faithfulness to the events is maintained to the maximum, and that no exaggeration or overwriting creeps in. Since the material is so horrific and mind blowing, it requires no adornment of decoration or supplementation. What is demanded is accuracy and optimal narrative spareness. His central characters, Sonia, Daniella, Piepel, and particularly Harry himself, are implanted into the scene, where the distinctions between fiction and documentary merge into a cast of *écriture* appropriate to the Holocaust itself. This writing is naturalistic, but not overblown, and certainly not sensational. This surely is not kitsch, but belongs to the nature of the material. This is a material not invented by the author, but found in place and demanding representation. Thus, the author is not seeking a *nom de plume* but an absent collective voice for a shared experience which must be rendered for a readership that must know it, if there is to be knowledge of what happened here, and how it was experienced.

It is as difficult to assess Ka-Tzetnik's work aesthetically as it is painful to read. Critics have sometimes charged the author with falling between the two stools of documentary representation and fictionalisation. But we have seen that the structure selected is fictional, although the general objective is to remain very close to the events represented, whilst sometimes adopting fictional names of places and persons. Thus, we have an interweaving of fact and fictional device, whilst the reader always remains clear about which is which. The whole opus constitutes an excruciatingly deeply felt and authentic document. It presents relentless horror at the edge of experience. For the reader, the evil is built in, incomprehensible for all our detailed familiarity with what happened, but of course known *ab initio*. In this sense, the work charts the chronicle of Jewish life in the twentieth century. This is such an innocuous sounding sub-heading, adopted by the author, but it holds such a devastating charge. There can be no happy end to the Ka-Tzetnik tale, even with the author's bare survival, and the transparency of the principal protagonist pointing to the author behind. This personal survival is denied, submerged into the consciousness of the millions of victims. The assemblage of texts then constitutes a chronicle, a document, and a source of information about the most terrible of multiple and continuing acts of criminality. We need it for its truth and to increase awareness of this history.

III

POET AND ACTIVIST: ABBA KOVNER (1918-1987)

Background

Abba Kovner was born in Sebastapol, in the Crimea. From 1926 onwards, he was living in Vilna, and then, under Nazi control, in the Vilna ghetto. On September 26th 1943 the ghetto was destroyed. The Jews were expelled by the Nazis, and Kovner went to the Rudinki forest, leading a group of partisan fighters there, following the death of the revered Itsik Wittenberg. He emigrated to Palestine/Israel in the wake of World War II from the new base in Italy. An organiser of illegal immigration under the British, he was imprisoned, then freed, and fought in the War of Independence. He settled on kibbutz Ein Hahoresh, where he lived until his death. A novelist, essayist, and, most notably, a poet, he has received the Israel Prize for literature. His life, rich in experience, so powerful and traumatic, informs all his writing. This body of work constantly poses the question: how is it possible to remain human in this cruel world?

Early poetry

He made the genre of the long poem, the 'poema', a form peculiarly his own, and he is almost unique amongst his young contemporaries, those Hebrew poets who started writing within the context of the Israeli State, i.e. post 1948, to adopt this genre, and then to deploy it as the primary mode of expression. His first venture into book publication was the long poem, *Ad lo or,* 1947 (Until No Light),[1] which constitutes an evocation of the partisan fighting. Later poems recall the other and subsequent war, the struggle for an independent Israel in the Middle East. But whether the scene is a forest in Byelorussia or Lithuania, or the territory that was to become Israel, the poems, as already noted by Binyamin Hrushovski[2] are not primarily narrative.

Had Kovner merely wanted to tell the story of the events, he would have adopted a different mode (as he did indeed in his prose work, *Panim el panim,* Face to Face). But the poems here are evocative not narrational; there is more drama than storytelling. Here, he attempts to present the feeling of an embattled fighter, although as far as Europe is concerned, the fighter is engaged in an unequal struggle, challenging an enemy overwhelmingly powerful, and the odds are hopelessly uneven. It in the later stages, in the fight for the Israeli State, that we approach the situation of some sort of 'normal' war. This is recorded in the sequence of poems, *Pridah mehadarom* (Separation from the South, 1949).

As Kovner says in the preface to *Ad lo or,* everything in the poem is not written as allegory, but as '... pure symbol, the symbol of Fate.' The writing is presented in the first person and from the

---

[1] References to Kovner's poetry are taken the edition of his collected poetry, *Kol shirey aba kovner,* 3 vols (Jerusalem : Mosad Bialik, 1996).
[2] See his three part essay in *Masa,* 1952.

point of view of the first person. The narrator is thirsty for revenge. But his feelings are also akin to erotic lust, although in this case the lust is for the destruction of the railway lines held by the hated Nazi enemy. That other love is contrasted with the utterly pervasive presence of death. It is not the separate incidents that have to be presented, accurately, scrupulously, and in perspective, historical and social, but rather the feeling of the writing individual, expressing his authentic being and sense of the moment. The focus of Kovner's poetry is not so much that hated other, the enemy, but rather the Jewish partisan himself, the hero of the poem/story. His survival is sought, as well as the longing for mother touch. An attempt is made to recover the sense of that struggle and persistence, although, perhaps indeed because, the voice has been silenced.

The long poem is not lyrical, not narrative, and not balladic. Streams of the Modern enter this long poem, Expressionist and Surrealistic. In the recent Hebrew tradition, the long poem had been written by such major practitioners as Abraham Shlonsky (in for example his war poem, 'Dvay' (Sickness), by Natan Alterman in such ballads as 'Simhat aniyim' (Joy of the Poor) and 'Shirey makot mitsrayim' (Songs of the Plagues of Egypt), also by Yitzhak Lamdan (*Masada*) and by Uri Zvi Greenberg (in most of his early Hebrew collections).

The necessity perceived by the poet in the adoption of this very specific and relatively unusual genre is to concentrate the total story into one emotional perception, to present something extensive but unitary. The object was to present not the specific, but rather the essence. The central figure of this collection is specifically, although anonymously, known by the single appellation, 'the partisan'. The tone deployed in the raising up of this figure is one of exalted pathos. The fighter bears the garland, now anointed, on his brow. The language used is religious and messianic: 'a commandment', and 'the primary sanctification belongs to the fighter'. But the second chapter (as in many long poems, the work is sectioned off, as in a novel, into chapters) heralds a new figure, that of the (still anonymous) woman. She is the second person addressee, an object of intense, erotic yearning. The passion of the writing is evenly placed at the edge of love and death, and there is a constant awareness of the proximity of separation to attachment.

It is interesting that a further long poem of Kovner's, 'Hamafteah tsalal', 1950; 1965 (The Key Sank), did not receive much attention on first publication, but then was republished in a collection called *Mikol haahavot*, 1965 (Of all the Loves). As a statement derived from past experience, it constitutes a summation of attitude. It is not only a narrative, but also a conclusion. A dialogue is conducted, specifically between 'mother' and 'daughter', in which the latter brings up the camp, following the disaster. But the only message that can be justly transmitted is one of resignation, the acceptance of defeat. The final words are: 'the end of it all is/ We are all defeated./ The dead and the living.' (178) Little satisfaction can be gained on any count. The language is symbolic. Ravens appear, hungry for the prey, and then, higher still, hovers the eagle. The mode is heroic, and the hero, of his nature, stands out from the crowd, 'facing the thousand.' Still, the mother is in the background, although his own view of the scene diverges from hers, as it does from that of the others around. What is stressed above all is the sense of the isolated one, holding his own, alone. But he is explicitly not a redeemer, and he does not come on a 'white horse'.

This collection was notable in Kovner's bibliography on two counts. Firstly, it was the first collection of discrete and therefore short poems, rather than the long poem ('poema') genre which the author had developed. Secondly, it was his first serious attempt to write love poetry.[3] The integration of love and war thematically, as well as the integration of the formal qualities of long and short poems, represents an attempt by Kovner at a holistic expression. The elements of violence (destruction, hatred) and love seem to be irremediably preclusive and opposite. But in order to inhabit a single universe, the poet looks for a unitary frame. The experience of the past is incorporated into the obsessions of the present in order to render a satisfactory account of life. Pictorial imagery and formal, modernist tendencies deployed here for the first time, also become part of the poetic confrontation with the contemporary world. Much has happened to the author over a relatively short period; the move from suppression and guerilla warfare to conventional war, the change of landscape, the transformation of the Jewish minority condition of oppression to Jewish sovereignty, and the casting of Hebrew as an official and majority language of State. It seemed that a new poetics was also to be called for. But the poet is always careful to remind us that he was aware of the classic Hebrew literature of the past, and that he was also trying to accommodate the contemporary idiom into the ancient *piyut*.[4] The past and the present were to become one, and he was also concerned to be a writer of current relevance and technique. There is a long tradition of lament as a discrete genre

---

[3] This volume, together with the volume, *Ahoti qtanah* (*My Little Sister*, 1967) won the prestigious Israel prize for the author, establishing him as one of Israel's leading poets.

[4] See S. Luria (ed.) *Aba Kovner. Mivhar maamarey biqoret al yetsirato* (Tel Aviv, Hakibuts hameuhad, 1988), 19, where, in an interview, Kovner says of the poetic forms in this phase of his work: 'These are forms taken from ancient verses (piyut), such as the 'cone' (gavia) form. But this is not just an external feature. The form is involved with labour, and there is the intention hold the time in which I live in these ancient forms. Such forms are adopted as it happens for the more brutal poems that express the modern era. This is an attempt to synthesise two opposite poles which are not amenable to synthesis. But this is the bridge.'

(the *qinah*) in Hebrew poetry. We find it early on, in the Bible, in the prophetic literature and in the Book of *Lamentations,* for example. Then again, in late antiquity and in early mediaeval poetry it is a common form of expression. Here, Kovner resurrects it in his memorial poetry, in *Mikol haahavot,* 1965 (Of all the Loves): 'Heavens that have not stumbled, clean of smoke and of ashes./ Again they colour the floor of memory for my head - bless, O my soul,/ That of all the loves - I have preserved from being trampled underfoot a flower that has fallen/ Amongst the pages of the book./ Do not rebuke me.' Then, the speaker addresses the figure from the past, that person whose coffin will never be lowered from his shoulders.

The new poetry here is reflective, inward looking although addressed to the female other, conversational, indeed close to prose, idiomatic in language and tone. But the underpinning sense is tragic, as the female addressee, the beloved is never to return. The new idiom is a device for accepting the inevitable, and a key to resignation. There is a residue of the former entity, but it is a shadow: '[O]nly your returning shadow/ Exists. Never/ Will my hands touch you. Never/ Will your coffin be lowered from my shoulders.' (16) Two things emerge in parallel, also contingent on each other. One is that the past is always with us, and the second is that the original state can never be recovered. That original love is still with him, although its object is irrevocably gone. But the other always present element, and necessarily so, is of course the 'I'. Because it is this 'I' that bears witness to the events, and that has to record them, and be their wavering testimony. Who is this first person? He is the one who '[h]ates new furniture...where your fingerprints show not their imprint.' (28) He is the one who '[l]oves beautiful/ Legends, which are really legends,/ Where the wise men have not obliterated from their essence the wolf/ And the forest.' And he concludes in that poem: 'And believe it or not/ I was also there drinking wine/ Drinking and drinking without any desire/ To weep.' He is part of it, he was part of it, but he will carry on in this present life. So we know very little of his proven, external existence, just of his fixation with this woman. And we know even less of hers, even how much of his obsession is based on observable fact. As he writes in one poem: 'Of all whom I have espoused, only you have I known,/ Because it is you whom I have invented.' (31) We are treading a fine line between reality and fantasy. But there is an expressed wish to '[g]o/ In a straight line/ Back/ To the world.' (43) Previously, (in the poem), there was the 'cry' and the 'hope', and the poem is addressed to the 'master of dreams'. So, it looks like a desired move away from dreamland. But, on the other hand, it seems that it is precisely hope that is lacking. Why else would he want to prepare himself for a visit to the Vilna Gaon's grave? As he lacks for nothing materially and has a child, and his wounds have apparently healed, there seems to be nothing that he could require, except ... hope. (47) There is a constant thrust of potential danger, the fire that might burn him. (48) His feelings towards her are ambivalent, both violent and nostalgic, sensing her abandonment, and longing for her return.

Prose writing

In the early 50s, Kovner's attention moved from poetry to prose. But, as with his poetry, the writing reflected the major public events that had always preoccupied him. The early poetry had related the horrors and the sensibility, both of the Jewish genocide and resistance, and then of the War of Independence for the establishment of the State of Israel. The major prose work too, the two volume opus, *Panim el panim*, 1953; 1955 (Face to Face),[5] does not escape the events. It is for this reason that the reader, including the author himself, finds it difficult to fit into the normal categories of generic distinction. He is careful in his introductory words to make two disclaimers; the first, that this constitutes a history, and the second, that it is really a novel. What it does attempt to do, he says, is '...to relate something that time and place disdain. And although all the characters in the story are my own, these things really happened, here, recently, at the portal of own times. And it is one episode of the war of the people.' And he adds: 'Maybe I have touched coals.' So the author has both invented a story, whilst drawing as precisely as he can on live actuality. It is the two-part account of Israeli war, not a chronicle, but also not fictionalised, set around the lives of two people, Shlomit and Itai, taking as its starting point a truce in the fighting, whilst Itai is still in khaki. The strategy of deploying two major figures in the story serves to present the action not just from two points of view, but from contrasted angles, one from within the 'group' (*hevreh*), and one from without. Shlomit not only sees herself as not belonging to this kernel of young, newborn Israeli fighters, of whom her beloved is one, but as positively antagonistic to an exclusive kind of club that exerts claims on him to her own detriment and exclusion. And this is not solely a matter of seeing a division between the native born Israeli (the *sabra*) and the immigrant, as, at this moment of history, the majority were inevitably not native born. It is also a matter of a deliberately cultivated view of the exclusivity and quintessential nature of this core. Who belongs to 'us', and who to 'them'? Shlomit is not one of the in-group, as is Bruriah, the freckled 24 year old, who is celebrating her birthday. The hero of this group is

---

[5] Abba Kovner, *Panim el panim*, 2 vols. 1. *She'at ha-efes*. 2. *Ha-tsomet* (Tel Aviv: Sifriyat Poalim, 1955).

the specific fighting collective, at whose helm is the *Palmach*, the workers' activist arm of the *Haganah*. This was the Defence Force that was soon to be merged, with the declaration of the State of Israel, into the national army (*Tsahal*). The concerns here are military and exclusive, focused on the self-conscious element that would create the conditions for a new nation. In this way, a displaced exile could assume a sort of home, and still be fighting for a recognisable future. Although the time and place of the action described are specific, and they have their necessary historical locus, the issues are still up to date. The enemy is the same it is today, and the fighting, which is patchy and inconsistent, has its own momentum. Moderate Arabs are drawn into a swathe of hatred which had not previously existed: '... In the meantime the son of such and such a person is killed on the city border, and the brother of so and so has fallen victim on the wayside in a move of retaliation on the part of the Jews, so that now comes the turn of revenge, and both parties are now constantly armed, and you can no longer say whether one man's rifle is aggressive or defensive, and now it is apparent that the Galilee is not so distant from the Negev, and that city and village are mixed up together, and that blood, pouring down from the mountain into the valley, has a way of going back and bursting out from the valley into the mountain, and the lines are drawn, and there is war unto life and death.' (*Panim el panim*, vol.1, *Sh'eat ha-efes*, 77) The linguistic texture is rich, the sentence long, sinewy, balanced and epigrammatic, and the doctrine of war is reflective. The scene is viewed not exclusively from the angle of one of the parties to the conflict, and not only as seen by a Jew who fought in the resistance, and who is now trying to establish a homeland in war. It is also observed from outside of the fray, commenting on human behaviour in conflict, and on the force of those events. The sense of catastrophic disaster, destruction on an enormous scale, is palpable, as war fever intensifies, arms pour in, and the populations become convinced that, since total war is inevitable between the two parties, then each had better seize the initiative and become stronger so as to be assured of victory. The events described follow the United Nations resolution of 29 November 1947 in favour of setting up two separate States in the area of Palestine, one Arab and one Jewish. This seemed to give the green light to a war of suppression on the one hand, and to a struggle of deterrence on the other. At this stage, there is too a third party involved in the conflict, i.e. The British army, present as mandatory authority, charged with responsibility, inherited from the old League of Nations, to control the territory until May of the following year, at which point the successor States would take over. So the conflict is in effect three pronged, and the Jews, on their way to potential independent Statehood, were fighting on two separate fronts, against the British, in order to establish an independent and viable State, and against the Arabs, who wanted the Jews out, and the total area of Palestine to themselves. This is the material of the novel too, as well as the personal stories of those involved. We can also see here how the novel so closely follows the actual events that it can be read as chronological documentary. Except, that is, for the cautionary words of the author, and for the atmosphere of emotional, personal and imaginative overlay in which the writing is enveloped. The action moves not only forwards, but sideways too, seeing various areas and parties in the conflict. So there are many characters in the novel. We hear of a degenerating and almost desperate situation, where the *yishuv* (the Jewish pre-State settlement) is vulnerable to attack from all sides, and is virtually defenceless. They also see the British as siding with the enemy, thus constituting another hostile element. The prime movers in the narrative are also split, both amongst themselves, and as between conflicting strategic obligations.

As we see, even if it may be difficult to pronounce on the literal accuracy in the account of the fighting, it is clear that the intention of the work is to report the war in considerable detail. Does this intention sit comfortably with what is, at least in part, on the basis of the author's own cited statement, a work of fiction? Are the two equally legitimate but separate genres compatible? Some have seen the two directions as mutually preclusive. We can and even should ask: if these things, as he writes, '[r]eally happened', why is this then not a history, or at least a partial history? And, if this work is a story of the imagination, even if based on fact, recent, verifiable fact as it is, why is the work not to be regarded as a novel? This generic confusion or at least blurring, may well have contributed to a lower estimate of the work over time, as the reader/critic has had difficulty in setting up appropriate measures of judgment. We still do find difficulty in reading the work in the way that it deserves. It surely does impose problems for the reader with the accumulation of detail in battle, as well as with the proliferation of characters, in seeing the wood for the trees.

However, the urgency of the prose and the richness of its texture reflect the immediacy of the dreadful situation. And one of the differences between poetry and prose becomes manifest in the latter's attempt to convey the ongoing actuality. The details of the everyday conflict in its various loci are conveyed as literally as possible, unlike the studied but distant, controlled and universal tone of Kovner's verse. Episodes of the War of Independence which became emblems of iconic heroism in Israeli historiography and mythology are here described in all their gory and tragic detail, as lives are lost, mistakes are made, shortfalls in personnel and equipment bemoaned. The dreadful shortage of rifles and their inadequate nature put the *yishuv* at a dreadful disadvantage in the face of an enemy considerably superior in numbers and firepower. As the defence of what is to be the new Israel proceeds, the embryonic Israeli army also finds itself fighting the British, who challenge them, and impound their ammunition. Death is all around, and despair approaches. But the loyalties are complicated all around, and no one can ever be sure who is for whom and to what extent. Are the Arabs always irremediably hostile? Are the British united in their efforts to suppress the Zionist enterprise? The Zionists too are divided, and some are so extreme (the *Irgun* for example) that they are regarded simply as murderers by the focus group here. The story is of course told from the point of view of the Jews, and the narrator attempts not just to capture the feelings and emotions of the inexperienced young commanders, but also to enter into them, microscopically in the wake of the events described, moment by moment. But also, the current situation is also seen by several of the participants in the light of the European quagmire which they have just left. Of course, only two to three years have elapsed from one situation to the other. Both involve fighting desperately against a much more powerful, or at any rate, more numerous enemy, with the prospect of imminent death constantly at hand. The detail crowded into this prose account would be quite inappropriate to poetry, whose practice is distillation and reflection. But there is an excitement too in the prose. The enthusiasm, which is described as reaching poetic proportions (248), arises from the new situation in the wake of the United Nations declaration. This is that the Jewish offensive has begun, that it is well organised and systematic, that everyone has now been issued with a rifle, that they can take the initiative, and take the fight into the enemy camp. Czech armaments had arrived. No longer did they have to await the attack, and then just defend themselves. Victory was sensed, and it marked the path to the setting up of a Jewish State. But, in the meantime, the personal life also has to be led, fed, and gratified. And it is this integration of the personal with the external, political, military, that is the subject of this massive novel. Some of the narrative is conveyed in the first person, a device which, of its nature, brings the reader more into an identification with the feelings of the protagonists, even as they are being attacked. The political climacteric of the book is the defence of Jerusalem. The effort made to engage in the breaking of the siege of the city is symbolic as well as strategic, and it represents the struggle for the very essence and existence of the total concept of the Jewish State itself. But we also have the full horror of the war, the casual deaths, the indifference, the lack of care for the other, even for one's own fighters. Against this background, the love affair between Itai, the novel's central figure, and Bruria is played out, an affair that derives its tension not only from the war, but from Itai's betrayal of Shlomit. Itai does not, it seems, know his own mind, and he becomes increasingly confused with every attempt to clarify his own feelings.

A further turning point in this fateful war is described following dreadful campaigns where there are wounded soldiers everywhere, and general slaughter. As is stressed by our protagonists, war is a learning process for both sides, and the fighting takes on a changing character very suddenly with the ongoing, fluctuating situation. (262) For the moment, so unexpectedly, the advantage suddenly moves to the 'Israeli' side, with the Arab evacuation of Yazur, without a shot being fired. The new and dramatic turn of events is the wholesale flight of Arabs, the surrender of arms, and the creation on a mass scale of the refugee situation. Suddenly, large tracts of land, including the Negev desert, are open to the Jewish fighters. Shaul, Itai, Avraham, Zvi, and others, share the consciousness of the action, the war, and what is the making of history, in a very different literary construction from Kovner's poetic work. And so the author moves on to the second part of his account in this heavy, semi-documentary novel. The fighting moves into a new phase, more decisive. The Jewish State is declared, as an independent political entity, although this is reported indirectly to the protagonists. Swathes of territory are conquered, and, on one view, this could herald the close of war. But, now another possibility looms, and is voiced. Is it not the case that every 'end' is always another beginning? (25) For there follows the intervention of armies from fully fledged Arab States, especially the Arab Legion of 'Jordan', the populous and powerful Egypt, as well as Syria, Iraq and Saudi Arabia. The course of the war can be understood better, as the fighters see the need to clear the territory of the potential enemies, 'who are still sitting on our heads'. (48) Jewish settlements are seen as a security ring, and Arab villages as vulnerable sites. We also see new aspects of our chief protagonists; for example, the new Israeli fighter, Katyushka, as a survivor from Poland. The past is always invading the present. These flashes of past reality intrude in the effort not only to live the present, but to build for the future, to survive, to create career prospects, and to enjoy a creative life. The narrative problem is to present the situation of the consciousness and the ongoing internal dramas of the several protagonists, as well as the changing war scene. The solution is to relay the actual history and the changing fortunes of the war indirectly, as reported to the characters. Some sectors of the war front had been extremely problematic, such as the fighting near Jerusalem, North of Latrun for example, where territories were surrendered and ceded, and many sacrifices were incurred. We also hear of the desperate bid to halt the Egyptian army on its way Northwards, with almost no barrier on the way to Tel Aviv, eventually held at kibbutz Negba. All this, and more, is recounted in authentic detail, as on the part of someone closely involved in these phases of the fighting. For this reason we find it difficult, as did the author himself, to make a clear distinction between memoir and reportage on the one hand, and fiction on the other. Thus we hear of the involvements of the five Arab national armies, and of the Israeli conquests, now related to Zvi, laid up, sick, for the moment. So we have two narrative levels, presented simultaneously, one as of the participants, and the other, as of a, perhaps fictional, but shading into the autobiographical, auditor. But such writing is not only factual and representational, but deeply emotional too, given the enormous suffering involved. And the sufferers are not only those who fight, but also those who wait on the side, the mothers and the families, who wait to hear about what is happening on the ground. Kovner's prose language, like that of his poetry, is rich and multi-toned, testifying to a background steeped in the sources long antecedent to his immigration to Israel. And the doctrines and experience emerging from the text reveal much about the views on Zionism and Jewish destiny then prevalent. Why suffer, it is asked. And the answer comes in the form of a further question: is there any plausible alternative to the struggle for the homeland?

Later poetry

Obsessive themes return. The most haunting collection of poems, *Ahoti qtana* (*My Little Sister*, 1967)[6] again addresses the beloved woman, now a heroine of the resistance. The volume takes the form of the 'poema' once more, and the addressee is part solid woman and part myth. Kovner's translator and chief has written: 'It will be clear, at the end, that Kovner is writing one poem and that his poem (reversing the sense of Eugene O'Neill's autobiographical play) is a long night's journey into day.'[7] Certainly, that is

---

[6] Abba Kovner, *Ahoti qtanah* (Tel Aviv: Sifriyat Poalim, 1967; 1970).
[7] Abba Kovner, *A Canopy in the Desert. Selected Poems by Abba Kovner.* Translated from the Hebrew by Shirley Kaufman, with Ruth Adler and Nurit Orchan (Pittsburgh: University of Pittsburgh Press, 1973), xxi. The complete text of *My*

the aspiration. Both the course of Kovner's life and his movement (emigration and writing) shadow statements of progression and teleology. There is a movement charted from oppression to self-determination, from occupied and oppressed central Europe to Palestine, from guerilla fighting to conventional warfare, from subjugated Jewish community to independent State. Likewise in the poetry and in the prose too one can chart this intended direction. But the dead often overwhelm the living, just as the living act as the beacon for those who died. And in this volume the dead speak too, through the pathetic voice realised in 'My Little Sister'. He searches out the little sister, and he lends her his voice, in an attempt to build a bridge between himself and her over the vast chasm of time and place.[8] The poetry of Kovner, particularly represented by this most famous of his poems, is a kind of reaching out. *My Little Sister* is representative as well as special. Kaufman writes in the introduction to her book: '[t]he central fact in Kovner's life is his confrontation with the half-dead, half-crazed girl from the mass grave at Ponar. Her face haunts every line he writes. We never see her eyes, her features – we never know her name. But we hear her voice. And the silence after the voice.'[9] The voice of the little sister, eventually silenced for the poet/narrator, is mediated by him through his own words. But these words are framed by ancient Hebrew poetry, specifically by the Biblical *Song of Songs* and the ancient liturgical *piyut*, with its insistent rhythms, repetitions, and resonant assonances, with their Midrashic associations.

The sister is compared to '[s]peaking ash'; so she has a voice, but she is also the residue of what had been a fire. Thus she is saved in a convent, facing the nuns, '[l]ike faces of monuments

---

Little Sister is reproduced in English translation in this volume, and this has served as the principal source of the translations quoted.

[8] Ibid. Kovner's appendix to the volume, 214.

[9] Ibid., xv.

in a foreign city.' She is a 'dove', with a 'torn wing'. The poet then goes on to use the language of ancient *piyut*, familiar from the festival prayer books: 'Their palms were gathered /In supplication.' For the sister to get into the precincts behind the walls she has to ascend the ladder. The walls constitute a formidable barrier, and the ladder acts as a bridge, just as it did for the angels in Jacob's dream.[10] Only then could God appear to Jacob, and issue His promise and blessing. In section nine of the Kovner poem, God seems to be a more sinister, even potentially threatening presence, spying behind her back, whilst approaching. And now there is another God, with starving eyes, '[p]regnant with love',[11] tempting strongly in another direction. At this point, his memory (presumably, the memory of him) is crucified, and swept outside the fence,[12] and she 'plays' with another God. There is the constant presence and pressure of desire in the convent without the normal outlets of sexual release available. The temptation to mourn is specifically rejected by her, because of what 'others would say.' The parties to the imagined meeting projected are: the speaker, the sister/bride, and God. What happened to the covenant that had been supposedly cut between God and man? 'My sister sits. Beside her/ A small dish of honey! Such a huge crowd!/ The braids of the loaf/ Twisted by the father./ Our father, thank goodness, took his bread/ Forty years from the same oven. He never imagined that/ That a whole people would go up in the ovens/ And the world, with God's help, still go on.' The same oven for making bread and for burning people! Both sanctification and destruction. What on

---

[10] *Genesis* 28:12.

[11] There is an echo here of the famous poem by Bialik, 'haeynayim hareevot' (The Hungry Eyes), recounting the poet's fall from innocence when tempted by the erotic female.

[12] This is an idiom, reflecting burial practices, expressing rejection by the community, something equivalent to 'beyond the pale'.

earth is God doing? Could there be a more fragrant breach of the covenant? The sister/bride has been brutally betrayed.

We have: 'Nine Sisters drenched with pleasure,'[13] and little prospect for them or for the sister of fulfilment through human contact. His sister has become 'like a wilted tendril' (section 30), weighed down by frustrated potential. Still the poet searches her out, as does the male protagonist his beloved in the *Song of Songs*. But it seems that she is not destined for the normal course of life, marriage and death. Perhaps, it is suggested, she was never born, as her (our) mother mourned her who had not come into the world. The poem concludes with the invocation to 'my mother'.

The End as the Beginning

The last poems of Kovner were published posthumously in the year of his death. They conclude on the same note as they began, in the genre of the long poem, with strong Biblical echoes, particularly from *The Song of Songs*. Although Kovner, according to many reports, rejected the appellation applied to him of 'poet of the Holocaust', the primary motifs of his writing hardly changed, although they did move thematically, as they did autobiographically, according to a scale of three; a) Holocaust. b) Resistance, and c) War. The fateful and paradigmatic life of the author returns constantly as a golden thread in his opus. Although his later life is set out narrationally, sometimes in considerable specificity, it is always coloured by his earlier history, and the later events tend to derive their significance and resonances from the earlier, dramatic imprints.

---

13 The Hebrew term translated as 'pleasure', 'ednah', is associated with erotic pleasure, 'jouissance'.

In *Salon qetering* (Kettering Lounge),[14] for example, the narrative of the long poem is directly autobiographical; a description of his visit to New York, and his hospitalisation there, followed by his return home to Israel. In this 'poema', the decorative typeset is important, and it illustrates the subject of life and death, one overwhelmingly encountered in hospital. But its contemporary relevance finds its redoubled relevance in the theoretical refusal, or at least reluctance, to go once more 'under the knife'. To refuse to go under the knife was what the Jews were invited to do in the ghettos of Nazi occupied Europe. Once more, we encounter the credo and practice of Kovner's writing in his belief, frequently expressed, that poetry is a form of prayer. The 'hero' of the poem is both the narrator and the third person subject. But he also speaks in the first person plural, entering his belief that: 'Soon/ Soon we shall know/ If we have learned to come to terms with stars/ That are not extinguished with our death.' And the conclusion is: 'Whither now?/ It is still not yet noon/ Even. Yet a cloud has begun very slowly/ To cover the sun/ That he so longed for when abroad.' The 'he' is of course the narrator too.

The final collection of Kovner's poetry, *Shirat roza* (Rosa Poetry),[15] appeared posthumously, in the same year as the collection previously mentioned. This was the poet's last manuscript handed on before his death.[16] It takes the form of a parable. But once more, the writing hangs on the borderline between literal reportage and poetic embellishment. The 'poema' here treats of the narrator's mother and a Jewish king; so it partakes of both the world of metaphor in the parable and of the eventful life of the poet/narrator, here taken from the aspect of childhood. In poetic

---

[14] *Salon qetering* (Tel Aviv: Ha-qibuts ha-meuhad, 1987).
[15] *Shirat roza* (Tel Aviv: Sifriyat Poalim, 1987).
[16] See the publishers' note at the heading of the text.

terms, this work is probably the nearest that the author comes to the presentation of his life history, but again, conveyed in both imaged and literal terms. We have (the prospect of) death, the death of others dear to him, search for meaning, and longing.

Rarely in Hebrew poetry has there been such a frank engagement on the part of the author with the search for truth through a fearless and transparent encounter with his own life history. That Kovner has conducted this enterprise primarily by means of a somewhat recondite genre of Hebrew poetry also testifies to that author's engagement with the historical backbone of Hebrew poetry, its ancient and mediaeval liturgy, as well as with forms of the Hebrew poetry of the earlier part of the twentieth century. That Kovner, as poet, and in his writing, goes beyond what might be regarded as the delimiting notion of 'poet of the Holocaust' also places him in his desired and more universal framework of poet of the human fate. This fate especially marks out the Jewish fighter born into such turbulent times, and making such a spirited commitment to the reinvigoration of both collective and personal life.

IV

SECOND GENERATION AND ACTIVE PRESENCE:
SAVYON LIEBRECHT

Background

Savyon Liebrecht was born in Germany in 1948 to Holocaust survivors, and immigrated to Israel as an infant. She studied
philosophy and literature at Tel Aviv University and received the
Prime Minister's Prize for Literature. Her background, albeit considerably shrouded in silence and mystery, constitutes the back-
drop for a considerable layer of her writing and thrust of her work.
For although she has grown up ostensibly as a *sabra* (native born
Israeli), the unspoken underside of her existence has assumed major importance, sometimes explicitly, and more often, implicitly.[1]

Like so many narrative writers in Israel (such as: Appelfeld,
Oz, Yehoshua, Kahana-Carmon), her early work consisted of short
stories before the leap into longer fiction. She then branched out
into television drama, and, more recently, she has written a novel.
Her first work appeared relatively late in print (the first volume,
Tapuhim min hamidbar, (*Apples from the Desert*), came out in book

---

[1] See list of Savyon Liebrecht's books and translations in bibliography.

form first in 1987,[2] with many prints successively following its huge success, before republication in 1992), but since then, she has become increasingly prolific. She has treated a great deal of those who have suffered from comparative inaudibility in Israeli society in general, and from within Israeli fiction in particular; women in a male dominated environment, Arabs in a Jewish dominated economy, and Holocaust survivors within a context that has attempted to supersede the dreadful events of the past, and, in some respects, to act as though they had not occurred. Much of her writing is born out of a creative response to silence and the suppression of the significant. She has said that the typical behaviour pattern on the part of survivors is either total silence in regard to the traumatic events, or, obsessive repetition, in the form of constant verbal return to the scene. Liebrecht's characters embody either or both of these, sometimes on the part of one person whose responses are catalysed at a particular life stage. Otherwise, various of her characters evince opposite reactions to each other, so that we might get the impression that they stand in for points of view and attitude.

The writing here reflects the influence of the doyenne of Israeli women short story writers, Amalia Kahana-Carmon, with its short exclamatory sentences, the introspective interspersed with the retrospective, the attempt on the part of the narrator to grasp the fleeting emotional moment of a distant feeling, now seeking recapture. In the very first story of the collection, 'Al qav ha-maagal' ('On the Line of the Circle'), the woman narrator faces up to a renewed meeting with the partner who had left her years ago without the explanation that she had then demanded. But now she realises that that explanation had been an attempt to block his

---

[2] *Tapuhim min ha-midbar* (Tel Aviv: Sifriyat Poalim, 1986; New edn. Jerusalem: Keter, 1992).

abandonment, and tears had followed. Now, she realises two things; that such movement should never be impeded, and that, in the natural course of things, a circular movement would bring him back again, as these emotional narratives follow a cyclical pattern. The breakdown of communication is not explained, and the only commentary is clarifying monologue, an attempt to present the plot rather than to confront the other. The situation is left rather than analysed, and the two parties are allowed to retain their separateness. Much of Liebrecht narrative suggests the limits imposed on the ambition to reach out, to reach out to the other party in the attempted act of communication, and, thus, also to reach out successfully and meaningfully to the reader. Experience may be an essentially private mode, first person in sense as well as in grammar, an experience that is private, and therefore misconstrued when communication is attempted. And which then may well misfire in the attempt to put into language what has been boxed into feelings.

An obsessive revisitation of the past is recorded in such stories as 'Ha-album shel ima' (Mother's Photo Album),[3] when Dr. Yehoshua Hoshen reflects on the way that there seems to be no record of 'the bad days' in his album. But, in his hospital, when he inspects his schizophrenic mother's medical record, the photograph that he attaches tells him of a shared and distant past. This brings to mind his mother's insistence on preserving this souvenir. The war years in Poland had shattered her life, both directly and indirectly. Later, her husband had left her, when he discovered that his first wife, whom he had assumed dead, had in fact survived. So he joined her in the USA, abandoning his later wife, the doctor's mother, to her present condition. The invasion of the present by the past constantly recurs, and it disturbs the patterns of attempted

---

[3] *Sinit ani medaberet elekha* (Jerusalem: Keter, 1992), 25-32.

communication between individuals who can not access the other's experience.

That this theme of attempted communication, as well as its failure, dominates Liebrecht's writing, we see in her later volume, *Tsarikh sof le-sipur ahavah* (On Love Stories and other Endings, 1995).[4] The first story in the volume, 'Parah al shem virjinia' (A Cow called Virginia), enters the mind of a mother joining her son, who had departed some years previously for Virginia. Not only was the geographical distance enormous, but the emotional distance between mother and son had grown apace. Now, with her arrival at this strange location in a desperate attempt to persuade him that his rightful place was by her side taking over the homestead in Israel. Now she discovers that the distance had been compounded by the added gap brought about through his entry into a ready made family, including a partner whose second marriage is to a Negro, (still married), and the children of both. Her first thought is to take flight and return home. Only then is she persuaded to meet the family, where the son, who is part Negro, had prepared his own 'farm' with Hebrew names. Enchanted, she can now be reconciled to a world of apparent differences, later reconciled. Initially, there had been no dialogue, only an interior monologue, which, of its nature, is conducted with no interlocutor. The meeting invites misunderstanding and conflict; their worlds had separated, and, in his view indeed, they had always been distant, although this distance was not acknowledged. The new approach, a kind of attempted revision of the script, can only be facilitated by an emotional openness, facilitated by warmth and then love.

---

[4] *Tsarikh sof le-sipur ahavah* (Jerusalem: Keter, 1995).

Memory Suppressed

Liebrecht has dealt in her fiction with the effects of the suppression of traumatic memory, specifically in relation to the horrors of the Holocaust and the Second World War. The process is two way; there are those who bear the memory, and there is the environment of the auditor/s, who might well wish to reject any such suggestion of that other world. In the story 'Hagigat haerusin shel hayuta' (Hayuta's Engagement Party) in the volume, *Tapuhim min ha-midbar*, it is the grandfather, Mendel, who is said, by the 'objective' narrator to bring disgrace on the family. The principal focus of consciousness is Bella, Hayuta's mother, daughter of Mendel, who acts as a shuttle between the two generations. On the one hand, she is to some extent sympathetic to her father, to his history, and to his efforts in the past to nurture the granddaughter. But, on the other, she dreads her daughter's fear of disruption, and her insistent demand for a smooth passage. She also feels she has to be accepted by the socially superior family into which her Hayuta is marrying, and does not want to be seen as a pariah. The daughter first wants to exclude her father from the celebration, a radical slap in the face that seems to go too far beyond the mother's spirit of compromise. Mendel's behaviour had radically altered: 'Up until six years ago he never said a word about what happened to him in the war ... A secret door to the memories of the war – what had been shrouded in blissful oblivion for decades – suddenly burst open forcefully. It all started on the eve of Rosh Hashanah.' But then, Mendel seems lately more and more to be drawn into spoken reminiscences of the horrors of the past, and these are particularly triggered by the sight of abundance of food and luxury. The compromise arrived at is that Mendel should come, but only on the assurance that he remain relatively silent. At the party, all seems to be going well, until the moment when he again seems to be on the point of raising the past. The family's abrupt intervention ensures not only the interruption of the speech, but also the final moments of Mendel. His collapse denies him the moment of 'final release'. It seems that the two realities cannot be sustained together. What we have is an observation about memory, suppression, suffering, and, also, subterfuge and pretence. Generations deny each other, even when they have derived their own sustenance from the rejected source.

Another such story is 'Kritah' (Cutting), from *Susim al kvish gehah* (Horses on the Highway). Here, the third person narrator tells of the grandmother, Henya, vigorously, almost violently, cutting off her granddaughter's hair, for fear of lice, which have been spotted by the schoolteacher. We soon discover that this act of 'cutting' is an acting out of repetition compulsion learned from the moment of liberation at the camp. But the reaction of Henya's son, and then, more hysterically, of the daughter-in-law, puts Henya's activity into the category of deligitimised madness. Children, she insists, should hear of Cinderella, not of Auschwitz. The story ends, not with the pursuit of the episode, but with a flashback to the source incident and suppressed memory, when the lice are expelled from her own head, and seek out new pastures for themselves. Again, the two levels cannot be accommodated together; the *soi-disant* comfort of the reconstructed Israeli life, with the protected children, and the not so distant history of the older generation.

Communication with the Past

The title story of the volume, *Sinit ani medaberet elekha* (I'm Speaking Chinese to you),[5] relates the private world of the individual and its refraction off others. The mother of the principal character, the elegant woman who turns up at the estate agent's office in apparent search of a suitable apartment, constantly echoes these words in the ears of her father. Her father, as recalled by the lady, had tried to show his love and desire for his wife, particularly on that vividly recalled day, when she had just turned fifteen. It turns out that the flat the woman is actually interested in belies her present affluent situation. She is in search of the apartment of her childhood, site of the childhood memory of her mother's frigidity and refusal of her husband's advances. All that had preoccupied her was the sight of the apparent stains on the ceiling. The 'Chinese' that she had been speaking to him was the plea for their removal, and his obstinate inability to correct this defect. The girl of that time, now an elegant lady, has returned to the scene, and can do her own bit to remove the past by returning to the scene of the initial fear, reencountering it in order to reverse its implications. What had been then a venue of repression, sexual fear and inhibition, now turns into a place of eroticised freedom. She seduces the estate agent, puzzled, overwhelmed and excited by the approaches of this lovely woman. With the satisfactory culmination of this act, the devils of the past can now be expelled. The woman is released from her past, from those fears. The sex is normalised, the 'stains' can be seen in proportion, the mother can be seen for what she is, and her own life can resume its appropriate path. The story brings together layers of time, which are also layers of life, and the past interplays with the present. Only one brief image of the parents'

---

[5] *Sinit ani medaberet elekha* (Jerusalem: Keter, 1992).

connection, 'bound together by war' and the daughter's recollection of the father's words, 'Even after the war, when sometimes I couldn't tell a woman from a man, only she, with her grey eyes – like a butterfly', suggests that her parents' lack of communication and mother's sexual aversion is bound to Holocaust trauma.'

As we see, much of Liebrecht's work presents the reader with these various layers of reality. The reader is confronted with one surface, which is the apparent reality. That is the picture as immediately viewed, the version, for example, that the estate agent of the story observes when the 'client' enters his office in all her finery and control. The other layer seethes beneath, and can in fact be decisive in the shaping of this woman's destiny and ultimate fulfilment. The parties to this are her two selves, that of the present and that of the past; firstly, her mother as remembered from then, secondly, her father as recalled in his romantic infatuation, despite all the obstacles that he has to overcome in relation to her mother, thirdly, the estate agent, who actually does come into his own in his capacity as 'agent', that is, as the instrument for the implementation of her will, and, finally, the apartment. This apartment had taken on mythical proportions as a source of dread and sin (the stains), and also as a source of fascination and introduction to the adult secrets. Now, it can be seen in another light, and restored to what it, to what it is as seen by the agent, as a rather inferior and dilapidated construction, not worthy of her consideration. She can be happy, and she tries to reassure the agent of her affection for him.

The Suppression of Women

One of the themes that comes up frequently in Liebrecht's stories is the position of women vis-à-vis men. This also intercuts with the recurrent holocaust theme, where it acquires its most extreme expression. But the settings are various and broadly imagined, from 'Westernised' scenarios in contemporary Israel, where the woman is still very often the junior partner in a relationship with the man, who makes the vital decisions, to the totally patriarchal Arab society, where the female hardly exists as an independent entity, and then to ultimate subjugation and sadism to which women were submitted under the Nazis.

An example of the first is the story, 'Eshet ish' (A Married Woman),[6] where the newly divorced Hannah has to face the rebukes of her adolescent daughter for not adopting a stronger line with her playboy husband. She defends him as rather being weak, and subject to the ministrations of artful women. As so often in the author's narratives, the past intersects with the present, flashbacks of their first meeting in Warsaw intercut the current sadness. She, however, has to remain faithful and loyal to the person that she had loved so dearly. In 'Hesed' (Mercy),[7] in the very short space afforded, we have a highly complex scenario of a woman, Clarissa, who is Jewish, had been raised in a monastery as a Christian to save her life, and who, after emigration from occupied Europe to Israel and a kibbutz, converted to Islam to marry an Arab from Hebron. Her present dreadful plight is that her daughter, Aysha, had run away, and will no doubt be trapped by her vengeful son-in-law. She is left with the daughter's illegitimate baby, born of her lover, whom she, the loving grandmother, now

---

[6] *Tapuhim min hamidbar* (Jerusalem: Keter, 1992), 115-119.
[7] *Sinit ani medaberet elekha* (Jerusalem: Keter, 1992), 93-100.

cradles and drowns. In protecting her from male potent cruelty, she exercises her own form of power. In 'Boqer ba-gan im ha-metaplim' (Morning in the Park among the Nannies),[8] horrific memories invade a present moment of a woman amongst carers tending the needs of infants in a play centre. She delivers an imaginary address to a young woman, whom she remembers (is this an accurate memory?) as a beautiful victim of German officers. She had been under the protection of a German officer, who had been genuinely good to her. But when that man died, she had been terrorised by the others. The climax of the story comes when the heroine of the story finally addresses the young woman, whom she had assumed to be the mother of the child that she was tending. But there has been a mistake. This is someone else's child, and she was just another carer. The reader might find difficulty in disentangling fact from fiction, or reality from fantasy, in the consciousness rendered.

Conflict and Resolution

Much of Liebrecht's narrative, short as most of it is, covers swathes of time. This time often sees change and reorientation, a new view of life emerging from the experience of years of seeing. Conflict, even enmity, lies at the heart of the characters' feelings. In the story, 'Katuv be-even' (Written in Stone)[9], the focus of consciousness is Areela, the widow, whose husband, Shlomi, had died in war on the Day of Atonement. Not only was she left in mourning, but for years following, his family never forgave her for taking

---

[8] Ibid., 83-92.
[9] From the volume, *Susim al kvish gehah* (Tel Aviv: Kineret, 1988), 71-86; (New edn. Jerusalem: Keter, 1992).

him away from his enclosed, religious life. According to this view, she had condemned him to death. But then, in an incident of memorial, many years later, his mother handed her a letter from the deceased that had been addressed to her shortly before his death. Areela's subsequent fury at the act of withholding, and the virtual theft of very private property, is then modified with the mother's half formed request that the young woman abandon that past, which is death, and seek a new path, which may be life and life. The new child which she is now carrying in her womb should not be called after Shlomi. She should take off his ring, and then stay away from the place of the old family. Here, the short story form is used in all its compactness to point to the change and subtle development that may take place over years, that also heralds radical transition. Conflict has become enlightenment.

Another possibility of shift is indicated in another important subject raised in Liebrecht's work, in the meeting of Arab and Jew. In the story, 'Heder al ha-gag' (Room on the Roof),[10] we have a meeting unexpectedly contrived through circumstances of work. The story concerns a new mother, whose husband, Yoel, is called away to work in Texas for two months. But, in the meantime, she had insisted on having a room built on the roof, an extension to the apartment that would have to be implemented in the absence of the 'master of the house'. Three Arabs turn up to carry out the work, and what is noted *ab initio* is only that they seem to be identical in appearance and unwashed. There is an apparently unbridgeable gap in culture, hygiene and development. This is expressed for example on the level of language, as their Hebrew is basic, functional, and limited. But one of the workers seems to take charge, and to assume a closer connection with her than allows her to feel comfortable. The border between the two sets of

---

[10] 'Heder al hagag' in *Tapuhim min hamidbar*, 42-61.

protagonists becomes unclear, as the workers move into the apartment for their eating arrangements. Then, it appears that Hassan, the one apparently acting as spokesman, had started to study Medicine, and that his English is more assured than hers. The language shift indicates a seismic movement, as his humanity breaks through, and the borderline between the two parties becomes further blurred. And, although the three workers had appeared indistinguishable at first, now their separate features can be clearly discerned. The place of imagination and fantasy in the primary character's world increases, and it may be hard for the reader to discern what is actually happening, and what she thinks is happening. There are conflicts in matters of job definition, in regard to payment and in regard to the job itself. But who is right? The borderlines, so insistently demanded, are crossed. Are the two parties separate entities, or can they be part of the same human block? She wants to regard them, and particularly Hassan, with affection. But she is also terrified of the implications, and so draws back sharply, in such a manner as to frighten him off. He disappears from the scene. Then, Yoel returns to find the work complete. For a summary of the events, a plot which concerns attitudes and emotional subplot, she begins to recount the goodness of the workers and Hassan's own warmth. But she then corrects herself, and tells Yoel of the (real or imagined?) chicanery of the employees, and adds, at the story's conclusion: ' "Arabs, you know…" ' The status quo seems to have been restored, but we have been through an emotional sea change.

There is a considerable degree of exposition in Liebrecht's stories. We, usually through the intervention of the omniscient narrator, know pretty well all that is going on, and it is translatable into consciously formulated language, in the minds of the chief protagonists. We are told of situations that project conflict, extension, development, and then, potential resolution. The sources of conflict might well relate to generalised stances and divisions in society. There is a colonialist situation in regard to Jews and Arabs in Israel, where the Jews play out the role of the colonisers, and the Arabs the colonised. There is a situation of religious tension as between the secular and the observant, the former of whom might be the Westerners (Ashkenazim) and the latter Easterners (Sefardim). And there is a sexual tension as between men and women, where it is often the latter who are more aware of the explosive implications of the erotic, electrical charge between male and female. An exemplar of this last tension is the story, 'Ba-derekh le-seeder siti' (Road to Cedar City),[11] where the woman, Hasida, feels that she is confronted by hostile elements, viz. the males in her family, her husband and son. Although it was she who had initiated and orchestrated this American trip, and had always tried to mediate between the two when the husband had been so angry with the son, they had now, it seems, ganged up on her, and made her an object of ridicule. We see again how there is deep hostility to be found in the most unexpected places, even in the bosom of a well-organised family. And we see it characteristically from the female point of view. And the place of fantasy is as strong as ever, where the related dreams act out her unarticulated fears and dreads. The dreams tell of the time when her husband was her true lover, and her child was hers alone. The tragedy is that this situation no longer pertains. Her fantasies are of their desire to be rid of her, so that her husband can be together with his secretary, and her son make free with his girlfriend. In the actual narrative however, there is a dramatic development. The Israeli couple with whom they are to be linked turn out to be Arabs from Jerusalem, the Hadads. This hilarious and tragic plot is complicated by the fact that their driver has no idea of the implications of the mixed

---

[11] 'Baderekh leseeder siti' in *Susim al kvish gehah*, 43-70.

background of his passengers, and talks incessantly about war and the glories of Israeli military achievement. Gradually, the fury of the Hadads builds up. But when they stop for a break it is Mrs. Harari who decides to help the child of the Hadads and stay with them on their minibus. The father and son will wait for another vehicle. She wants to breathe freely. In this beautifully executed story, heroic Israelism is turned on its head, and made synonymous with egoism, chauvinism and machoism. The woman backs out, seeking out the other woman as her travelling companion.

A Man, a Woman and a Man

The movement out of the short story form represents not only a shift of genre, but also the broadening of a search. A novel is not only longer than a story; it also combines more threads, and the investigation of a personality on several levels. It also allows for the plot to develop in more complex ways. We have seen that a major theme of Liebrecht's writing is the difficulty of communication. From the vantage point of an individual, a woman, the 'other' is seen as at least potentially if not actually hostile. But communication is essential for human life, and in its ultimate expression, it is love. This is the theme of the novel, *Ish ve-ishah ve-ish* (A Man, A Woman and a Man).[12] An initially chance meeting takes place between a woman coming to see her mother in an old age home, and a man, similarly attending to his helpless father. In her first attempt at extended narrative prose, Liebrecht sets up a complex scenario. The woman is taken up with sympathy not just for her own mother, and not just indeed for the other man's father, in even worse state, but for the condition that befalls all. Her husband

---

12 *Ish ve-ishah ve-ish* (Jerusalem: Keter, 1998).

though, to whom she confides these anxieties, has no time for all this, and just moves on to his own immediate preoccupations. A now familiar theme crops up; the woman, Hamutal, feels excluded in her own environment, this time, by her husband and by her daughter, who is much closer to him than she is to her. The background accumulated in a novel can be much more detailed than in a short story, with more exposition and specifics. Here, the prior information and background that the reader receives allows for a certain implicit insight into apparently aspects of Hamutal's behaviour. This behaviour is noted by the husband and daughter, but Hamutal herself feels helpless and at the mercy of blind forces leading her in random directions. We are given the history of her mother's sexual repression, and then see the explosion of frustration in her senile erotic fantasies. The primary subject is the horror of aging, and this is what links the two principals in the novel, both of whom have senile parents in the same institution, both of whom had been sparkling individuals at an earlier stage of life. The biographical background of the dramatis personae is elaborated, and the attachment between the principal protagonists can develop naturally and gradually. But the plot is also moved on by the element of fantasy, and through the agency of related dreams (Hamutal's work as an editor revolves around a periodical issue devoted to nightmares). Both of them also keep projecting themselves into the skin of their parents, seeing themselves in their situation, mindless and helpless, terrorised. Several questions are raised by this study of relationships. The stance towards her mother on the part of the heroine is formative, and we may ask whether this virtual obsession with the mother in such dramatic decline may not be a kind of revenge for the lack of love received by the child. Now she can observe the parent in her weakness. But what is further raised is the underlying and persistent nature of the Holocaust background, and now the adult's ability to reinterpret things seen in the distant child past. This background had, typically, been suppressed by the mother, who had not verbalised the events to the daughter, but rather redirected them in her insistence on discipline and ambition. This had resulted in distancing and lack of love, even of basic communication between the two generations. The novel climaxes with, first, the death of Saul's father, then, with his own emotional distancing from Hamutal. Then it continues with his actual return to Chicago, and finally, with the death of Hamutal's mother, followed by the reunion with her husband and children. The nurse at the Home advises her to 'return to life', and surrender the unwholesome preoccupations that have led her on to difficult and painful paths.

Can We Communicate?

Breakdown of communication, together with the effort of reparation continues to constitute a major theme in the Liebrecht narrative. In the novella, 'Ha-gever shel brigita' (Brigita's Man),[13] the first person narrator tries to teach her father some basic English, so that he may be able, even in his disabled state, confined to a wheelchair, to communicate with the Filipina whom she has hired to nurse him. He is, as he admits to his daughter, just 'rubble', i.e. useless, awaiting disposal. But as the pathetic degree of English that he can summon up is insufficient to make this new aid aware of his most elementary needs, the mother intervenes in her own dominating and effective manner. Each gesture, movement, and speech act is interlaced with the narrator's own interpretation. Gradually, a silent conspiracy of the ineffectual is woven between the narrator, the father and the nurse, against the mother.

---

[13] One of the three stories from *Nashim mitokh qatalog* (Jerusalem: Keter, 2000).

But the story gets complicated, and we are unsure of the newly emergent loyalties, as we are unsure of whether the nurse, Brigitta, is working honestly, or whether she seeks to exploit the situation. The old man is fascinated by her, but finally seeks her dismissal, perhaps embarrassed by his sexual proclivities which he wants her to satisfy. The narrator suspects her of duplicity, and then, through questioning of the apparently abandoned mother, discovers the background of her parents' unhappy marriage. It is a story then of loyalties and hostilities, of who is in and who is out. This is not so very different from the isolated, enclosed worlds of the survivor in Liebrecht's stories. The misdirection of language may not be attributed here to the Holocaust experience, but it remains a common human difficulty, located in the practice of interaction. So there may not be an irreconcilable path to interpretation in pronouncing upon the issue of the separate and incommunicable experience of the survivor, qua survivor, or qua human being.[14] The author could well be pointing in two directions, to the effect of the horror and the difficulty of its transmission, and also to necessarily private experience of the inner world of each person, which may well have something in common with the world of the survivor, with all the shades of difference that we have to respect. To this degree, experience requires a special language, or, at any rate, a language that is only completely absorbed and felt by the speaker.

Likewise the main character in the second story in the collection, Shulamit in 'Ha-yeled shel diana' (Diana's Little Boy), is incapacitated in her speech following the murder of her son by Arabs in the Golan. She declares that she will speak no more.[15]

---

[14] This point was taken up by Lily Rattok in her introduction to Savyon Liebrecht, *Apples from the Desert: Selected Stories* (London: Loki Books, 1998), 33, note 15, where she insists on the special nature of the Holocaust survivor, and the particular incommunicability of their voice with non survivors.

[15] *Nashim mitokh qatalog*, 85.

She retreats into herself, and refuses not only comfort, but any sort of contact with the outside world, with her family, and with her husband. Specifically, and most angrily, she turns against all Arab connections, and rejects the associations which she had nurtured over the years as midwife to Arab children, and with her extensive knowledge of the Arabic language and practices. But the Liebrecht narrative often reads somewhat like a case history, and here we have the beginnings of a therapy emerging with the complex dénouement. It transpires that Eitan's girlfriend, Yael, had taken a liking to his best friend. Partially perhaps in retaliation, Eitan had contracted another association with an Irish girl, who had then become pregnant by him. The resolution is that the best friend and Yael are to adopt the (as yet) unborn child. Once more, we have the pattern of insider crisis, breakdown of communication, outsider intervention, followed by reprise and new direction.

The third and final story in the collection, 'Ima shel valentina' (Valentina's Mother), also revolves around an outsider/interloper into a closed community. The disabled Paula Ostropovich in Israel receives a young nurse, Valentina, from Poland through the good offices of a local Priest. Initially, all contact is marked by grudging suspicion of the Christian, clearly nurtured by a background of prejudice and fear. The question raised here is: who is the outsider? Valentina is a Polish girl, a Christian, in Israel, but Paula is a Holocaust survivor, and now old, rejected by her family. Much of the story consists of flashbacks, to the time of the Nazi invasion of Poland, when Paula was just sixteen years old, the same age as Valentina now. So, a parallel emerges between the two, in their human situation vis-à-vis the collective. They even have the same memory, of a childhood melody. So Paula can seek the girl's friendship, and asks to be addressed in the familiar 'thou'. But the closeness gets out of hand and consumes her, as she begins to see the child as her own, and seeks her adoption. The insider group here is that of the Polish speakers, sharing common childhood memories and associations. Paula had forgotten all that had happened before the trauma of war had wiped it off her mind, and now it could return. The horrific and surreal conclusion of the two of them throttled by gas fumes, a murder and a suicide (though we do not know which is which), freezes them in their present positions. It is a strange way to relive the past.

The Nature of the Story

We may see that we, as readers, have gained in learning about detail with Liebrecht's novel, and also learned something of the essential disparity between long and short fiction. But we also may note that what we have gained in specificity, we might have lost in suggestivity. The plasticity, the terseness, and the unexpected turn, based on psychological observation and the analysis of interpersonal relationships, emerge brilliantly in the brief narratives. As we saw in her later volume of short stories, the author again deals with relationships, with assumptions made by individuals regarding others, and with sudden revisions. A new attachment is now possible. The point made by a Liebrecht story is to uncover what had hitherto been hidden. Just as in life individuals only discover facets of their personality unexpectedly, or perhaps through analysis or introspection, so fictional devices can lead to revelation. This, of course, is a source of narrative tension, and one of the enduringly appealing aspects of narrative fiction.

So the Liebrecht story is often marked by the unexpected twist, rich in plot and diversity. But the narrative turn is not arbitrary or conventional, but rather based on a fictive life taking over the direction of the narrative, and then directing it in a manner that illuminates both character, and then also life in general on a deeper level. By the end of such a story, we know more about the person involved, the life already lived, as well as the potential for further development. Although the end may be rounded off, lines may be observed for further movement. The sources of such movement; the Holocaust, an aspect of the past very much alive in the present, Israel's class divisions, the tension between Arab and Jew, the tension indeed between human beings as they move in and out of relationships, alliances and hostilities, the unequal balance between male and female. All these act as a catalyst for some of the most remarkable and arresting contemporary Hebrew fiction.

V

THE HOLOCAUST IN THE FICTION OF DAVID GROSSMAN

The Range of Grossman's Writing

Although David Grossman (b. 1954) was not born to survivor parents, and he himself is a native of Israel, the Holocaust has been and continues to constitute a major motif in his prolific literary output.[1] His work consists of documentary journalism, particularly concerned with the Israel-Palestine conflict, and of fiction, both short and long. One of the outstanding features of his writing is that much of his focus devolves upon the view of the child. This serves to heighten the sense of discovery and wonder. An ob-

---

[1] For a list of David Grossmann's books, see bibliography.
Grossmann's books in English Translation:
Smile of the Lamb (1991).
The Yellow Wind (1988).
See Under: Love (1990).
Sleeping on a Wire (1993).
The Zigzag Kid (1997).
Duel (1998).
Be My Knife (2002).
Someone to Run With (2003).

server, as it were, happens on an event for the first time, and becomes passionately interested in learning all there is to know about it. For an adult, such material may well be marked by familiarity and over exposure, whereas, for the child, it is necessarily seen afresh, as the range of his experience is so limited.

Such is the case for the two major subjects of Grossman's opus; the Palestine conflict and the Holocaust. They are also the basic themes that underlie contemporary Israeli existence. They provide the ballast and the *raison d'être* for the Jewish presence in the Land, as well as the major obstacles and difficulties. Israeli existence is problematic and tragic, as well as challenging and exciting. This is what Grossman attempts to convey, often through the eyes of a child protagonist, first or third person, in fiction rich in plot construction, as well as in racy journalism, based on the timbre of the human voice and the pain of experienced history.

We may ask if there is a literary common denominator between the two major historical concerns, and if they are linked by a unifying narratorial thread. There are of course in addition works of his in which neither of the two motifs is apparent, and yet pose similar interrogation. His autobiographical work, *Sefer hadiqduq hapnimi* (1991, *The Book of Intimate Grammar*, 1994), seems to reflect much of his own life and that of the child growing up in Israel. The play, *Gan riqi* (1988, Ricki's Garden), as well as *Yesh yeladim zigzag* (1997, *The Zigzag Kid*, 1997) and *Mishehu laruts ito* (2000, *Someone to Run With*, 2003), deal primarily the child, growing into maturity, and seeking adventure. These seem to be traditional examples of the *Bildungsroman* (a novel of the central character's initiation) in which the hero sets out in life to find out things for himself, armed with little experience and resources, and then emerges rewarded by experience and enriched by life itself. But this form is employed with unexpected and innovative variations in the author's great Holocaust work, *Ayen erekh ahavah* (1986, *See*

Under: Love, 1990). In this, the protagonist of the first lead-in section, the child Momik, sets out to discover the truth of what is known in his home as 'the Nazi beast', as well as the truth about what took place 'over there' (i.e. in those lands where the Holocaust raged). The factor in common between these diverse expressions, as well as in the journalism treating the conflict over the Land, is the issue of power. How does one person acquire domination over the other? How indeed does one group, or nation succeed in this endeavour, and how is this relationship of domination expressed? We see the tensions in the child world, particularly in relationship to the adult. We see it too in the imbalance between the Israeli and the Arab in the 'territories', i.e. The West Bank and Gaza, and we can observe it as well in unequal scales of Jew and Nazi in the course of the Holocaust years. What distinguishes Grossman's writing though is the author's attempt to analyse the phenomenon, as it were, to dissect the body, which is the relationship. Such a relationship exists, for the author, in the scale of obsessive love. Such love is, of necessity, unequal, lacking in perfect balance, and its nature is suggested by the metaphor of a knife penetrating the skin. In the epistolary novel echoing this metaphor, the chief protagonist, the man in *Shetihyi li hasakin* (1998, *Be My Knife*, 2002), treats his epistolary lover, Miriam, only seen and otherwise unknown by him, to a series of graphic letters, in which he invokes Kafka's letters to Milena, where Kafka writes that: '[l]ove is to me that you are the knife on which I turn myself.'[2] This sado-masochistic metaphor presents an image of what such a relationship might be like between the two who hardly know each other, one dependent and suffering, the other passive, necessary, and inflicting pain. Such a relationship is deeply unequal, reciprocal

---

[2] Franz Kafka, *Letters to Milena* (London: Minerva edition, 1992), 159. In the German edition, 187.

in an unbalanced manner, the manner of master to slave. But, as we shall see in much of Grossman's work, the master can be just as much dependent on the slave as the slave on the master. The significance then of other such structures in the author's opus, is that they may serve as template for a wide range of edifices, whether personal, national, historical, private or general. They serve too for Grossman's work in regard to the Holocaust. In the fantasy of both parties, the aspiration is towards unity, and indeed towards union beyond unity, where the two separate entities become merged into one. Thus, the sexual act is perfectly illustrative of this merger, the single function in which two people come together, and, for some moments at least, merge into one. Is that the relationship between torturer and tortured, between conqueror and conqueror? Is hatred thus akin to love? For the lover, in the Grossman novel, through his letters, love can lower all defences, to the extent that the normal bounds exerted by the constant censorship of everyday life are lowered: 'And I am making do without any makeup in my pursuit, without any censorship, and altogether without any self-defence.'[3] As he writes later, only when the artificial division between them be broken, '[c]an I feel that you will be you.'[4] Likewise, her ultimate wish, expressed after his many letters amongst the very few that are given to her, is that '[a]ll these thousands of words should become a body.'[5] (This seems, incidentally, to provide a commentary, as well as a resolution, to Kafka's desul-

---

[3] David Grossman, *Shetihyi li hasakin* (Tel Aviv: Siman qriah, 1998), 13. All translations are my own.

[4] Ibid., 256.

[5] Ibid. The conclusion of the novel.

tory and desolate statement, that he is made of words, a state that he would love to escape).[6]

See Under: Love

And so to Grossman's major Holocaust work, *See Under: Love*, which represented a major turning point in the author's opus in terms of dimension, form, subject matter and narrative variety. It is also his only work hitherto that is entirely and overtly devoted to the Holocaust, which constitutes the starting point and the thematic focus. Although Grossman had previously played with fictional form in his adoption of multiple perspectives in *Hiyukh hagdi* (1983, *Smile of the Lamb*, 1991) and with stream of consciousness in *Rats* (1983, *Running*), it was in this new and more substantial work of fiction that he was to adopt narrative approaches *ad seriatem*, both apparently moving away from the subject, and yet still facing it.

There are four sections in the novel. The first, called 'Momik', from which the following three take their bearings, can be deemed realistic. The second, 'Bruno' is dreamlike. The third, 'Wasserman', is fanciful. And the fourth, 'The Full Encyclopaedia of Kazik's Life' is factual and objective. No conclusion is reached, and there is no attempt to round off the narrative/s and come to some sort of climax. Momik, the nine year old child moving into adolescence, bears the narrative consciousness of the first section, although it is conveyed in the third person through the eyes of an outsider adopting a tone very close in spirit and content to that of Momik himself. Characteristically of Grossman the storyteller, the

---

[6] See Franz Kafka, *Letters to Felice* (London: Penguin Modern Classics, 1975), 428. He writes there: 'I have no literary interests but am made of literature, I am nothing else, and cannot be anything else.'

section opens by plunging the reader straight into the heart of the plot, with no preamble. We are told in the first sentence that Momik, on a specific date in 1959, received a new 'grandfather', presumed to be the Anshel Wasserman of the third section, sometime children's writer and unexpected survivor of the unspeakable horrors of the extermination camps. From the outset, the descriptive prose of the narrator merges with the speech of the protagonists to produce a continuous, monochrome narrative. The events are mostly witnessed by the child, or at any rate conveyed in his tones, although they still carry sufficient information for the reader to find his bearings. We are both in the Tel Aviv of that period, but also cast an eye back to the nightmare created by the 'Nazi beast'. In effect, we have three time frames within the section; the time of composition, which is the mid-eighties, the setting of the event, back in 1959, a date on whose precision the narrator insists, and the concentration camp setting itself, i.e. the war years. So the narrator dresses himself in the skin of the child Momik, a child in the process of excited discovery, gradually uncovering the truth about events whispered fearfully over his short lifetime. We can thus see the novel in its totality as a container of approaches, or in adult speak, as a packet of possible ways of sustaining life through the pervasive presence of death. The three experimental approaches exemplified in the successor sections can be seen as suggested solutions to the conundrum posed in the first section. The large question is why. And the answers come in the form of how; through Bruno Schulz in the sea off the port at Danzig (now Gdansk), through the persistent 'unkillability' of Wasserman at the camp, and then, most precisely, through the sourcebook of the encyclopaedia, purporting to embrace everything concerning the life of one person, Kazik, the fictional hero created by Anshel Wasserman. So, from the fiction of a character in the novel, we move back into fact. The narrator himself though is aware that he is being constantly lured away from the objectivity of fact into the subjectivity of direct speech. But if fact be the refuge here of fiction, so fiction is also the tool of fact. Anshel Wasserman, the hero of the total story, just as Momik is the focus of consciousness, is a supreme fictionist, as well as being the object of torture. That is his release, and also his memorial. As in the old Arabian tale of Sheherezade, fiction can still prevail.

In the actuality of Momik's story, also his history, Anshel is not his literal grandfather but his mother's uncle, whom he refers to for purposes of convenience as his grandpa. He must know this full well as he knows so many other things. Momik in fact is an excellent receptacle for all that passes, as, and this is said explicitly (11), so he can also fulfil a function as diarist and recorder. He records the devastation of the past through the human residue of Anshel, through his mother and her biography, and through the lives of those around which have been so damaged by the recent past. The Jewish tragedy is alive and present in its residual state, here in Israel, also composed of a residue, now attempting to regroup. Momik's observations are minute, recording what others would certainly ignore or forget. He is intent on two things, on the live drama now being enacted before his very eyes, and the adventure story that had been written by Anshel Wasserman, the very figure who has been resurrected, and who has now arrived to be with the family in Tel Aviv. Momik has found the old text of the Anshel's stories, which he is now recopying into his diary, and which we can now read in the quaint and somewhat archaic language of the original. (Anshel had been a Hebrew writer in Poland). As is the nature of children, Momik blurs the boundaries of the past. For him, the old newspaper column is as ancient as the scroll of the sacred Law, and is thus also sacred, particularly so in view of the exciting adventures related.

The blurring of the boundaries between fact and fiction is illustrated by the novel itself. The overt subject if the work is the Holocaust, which of course is known in and bound by the facts, figures and places of specific regions and periods. But that large and dreadful space has acquired mythical dimensions, and so enters not just history but legend as well. The child has known the space of the 'event' as the 'land of there' (*erets sham*, 17*ff*.). Events too terrible to be articulated precisely are mistily alluded to by the euphemism of 'there', which the child seizes on as a literal if magical area. Thus, that whole other experience takes on the sort of aura associated with the plots of the great writer, Anshel Wasserman, and a special vocabulary comes into being to summon it up, with such concepts as the 'land of there' and the 'Nazi beast'. There is an intermingling of childish dread at the evidently awesome experience and the difficulty that a child has with relative dates and places at some remove. This has clearly been reinforced as well by the reluctance of adults to articulate the memory, particularly in the presence of a child who should be shielded from such things. This leaves open questions which might otherwise have been easily resolved. For example, Momik is deeply perplexed by the numbers marked on the arms of members of his family, and treats them as though they are some sort of code which he resolves to break, certain that a deep mystery lies behind the combination, some sort of *gematria*. He discovers that Anshel's number will not be removed even after persistent scrubbing, so he comes to the conclusion that the number has been engraved from within. It is stressed that Momik has a scientific bent, and so believes that all phenomena have a direct cause which can be discovered by rational procedures. Momik inhabits not only a childhood world, inevitably, but also a very private world in which he can pursue leads that are only available to him. One of Grossman's greatest narrative talents is to present the world as a child would see it, very much from that angle, directly and unpatronisingly. For the adult, this constitutes an enabling device, so that he can revise material that might otherwise be over familiar and therefore banal.

Although Momik is presented as a living a child life and although indeed we read the third person narrative through a specifically childlike vantage point, Momik's consciousness is also permeated by the damaged adult atmosphere around him. He is the only child in the household, and the only person born in Israel, where all the others are survivors. They bear their scars still, acknowledged or not, and Momik has absorbed the damage without really understanding what has brought it about. In this sense, he exists on the margins of two realities, and he has to pick his lonely way into his own notion of enlightenment. It is probably in recognition of the inadequacy of the interpretative skills at his disposal that the narrative has to move into the other, non-realistic modes in order to proceed further in making sense of the given discourse into which he is plunged. 'There', the 'Nazi beast', the scars, the code words and names, the foreign languages, the cries, the hints, the significance of apparently innocent sounding words like *Links* and *Rechts* all derive from elsewhere, and impact on the Hebrew speaking child, native to Tel Aviv, as a source of powerful, dreadful, but fascinating mystery. The adults are of course all involved in their own conspiracy, which is to shield the child from their own experience. But this is only partially achieved, and presents an alluring aura which Momik seeks to penetrate. And he sees himself as a lone fighter in a campaign which would be thwarted by all these adults in the vicinity.

The beginnings of Momik's enlightenment lead from the first section of the novel into the later ones. Anshel is a link, and Momik describes him as a 'prophet backwards' (33), that is someone who speaks obsessively and exclusively about the past. The new arrival can clearly aid the child in the pursuit of understanding. Momik's objective is to translate adult metaphor into child literalness. He actually has to locate the 'beast', presumed to be at large in the cellar. They are apparently such a simple family, hard working, devoted to each other and quiet. But in fact they are all precariously balanced on the edge. Momik is constantly waiting for the disaster to come about, and is always relieved at evening mealtimes that another day has come to a close, as though that possibility had been in doubt. At any moment, there might well come a message from over 'there', with the 'beast' ready to pounce. The family is in fact quite out of tune with its environment, isolated and suspicious, quite unused to social life, mostly able to put a lid on their fears and panic. But then such anxieties burst forth. At night, the household can rock to the sounds of moaning. Strangers are held to be a source of terrible threat. And the family turns in on itself, a family within which Momik is thus doubly removed from the outside world. Momik is usually able to deal with Anshel better than any other member of his family, through his tolerance and curiosity. But there are occasions when Anshel bursts out of his protective shell, such as when, in his fantasy or memory, his camp torturer Herr Neigel, who constantly demands new stories and sequences to existing stories, seems to threaten to get into the story himself. But the story is Anshel's most intimate possession, and is uniquely and exclusively his own. Only Momik can empathise with this sensation. He is living in that same world. As he matures, beyond the nine years and a quarter at the story's opening, his questions get more urgent as his reading and knowledge of the Holocaust increase. But as the information, now forthcoming, is provided, so the problems pile up, demanding further answers and more knowledge. As a last resort, determined to pin down the beast, he takes Anshel himself down to the cellar in an attempt to confront the beast with a 'real' Jew. Surely, as the exemplar of an authentic Jew, he will lure the beast from his lair. And Momik brings in other people from 'over there' as well, old men whom the beast surely could not resist. But to no avail. Time passes, and Momik makes no progress. The adults decide that he must change school and leave the town for fresher climes and a healthier environment. Then, Anshel himself disappears, seemingly into thin air, never to be traced again. The whole of this episode extended over just five months.

And so to the sea, which swallows up a new hero, Bruno, that is Bruno Schulz the great Polish writer, casually shot by his Nazi tormentor in 1942. That is the historical Bruno Schulz, a writer of sketches, collected in two volumes, a caricaturist of note, and the author of a lost manuscript, with the title *Messiah*. His work was of such originality and power that Schulz entered the ranks of Polish literature as one of the great modern masters. But here, Grossman creates another possible Bruno, one who flees from his Drohobycz ghetto and escapes to the port of Danzig, pursued by the Gestapo. There he goes into the sea. This section apparently deviates from the thread of the other three. Momik had led on to Anshel, whose story is told in section three, followed by a final encyclopaedic discourse, in alphabetical order, relating all that concerns a hero of Anshel's fiction. The novel once more wavers between historical actuality and the possibilities inherent in fantasy. The narrator, who is now the adult Momik, intervenes to relate how in 1981, after receiving Schulz's stories, he felt that he had to tell of his life, which he insists did not end as a slave to the SS commandant Felix Landau, when shot by Landau's enemy, Karl Gunther, but carried a sequence. First though, he must tell of his continued determination to follow up the story of Anshel Wasserman through every possible source, through archives and old newspaper cuttings. But it seems that the story of Bruno constitutes a branch of this original tale. In order to write about the Holocaust he (i.e. the narrator) had to write about Bruno. And in order to write about Bruno he had to investigate his own life story in Poland itself, as near as possible to what had been known as Danzig. So, after extensive research into the period and place, soaking himself in the documentary material, he obtains the necessary permits (this of course is during the final days of Communist rule there). In answer to questions put, he says that he needs to stay in the region in search of the Polish writer, as Bruno was the one who knew how to fight those hostile forces, and all that had happened in reality (96). From the detailed description, mentioning well-known figures from Warsaw University, we see that although the narrator Momik is a literary invention, the account follows literal truth. Again, we have faction within a fantasy, and the intertwining, so characteristic of Grossman, of reportage and imaginative creation. Because then, in Gdansk, on the encounter with the sea, which the narrator addresses, the text following presents the speech of the sea herself [*sic*]. In psalm like tones, the sea recounts the moments of Bruno's own final submergence. This part of the novel is perhaps the most linguistically innovative, as is appropriate for the creation of a language fitting for such an ancient element, combining indeed antiquity and the recent past in an ongoing sweep of a continuous sentence. But we still have the interplay with the narrator's own discourse, reminding us of where and when we are. The venue for this section is the sea, an element and location which possesses a depth unequalled on land or in the air. A trialogue takes place, between the sea, Bruno and the fish, orchestrated and directed by the narrator. The narrative speculates on why the narrator is concerned to write about Schulz, and the same question could be put in regard to Wasserman. We discover that two heroes of the novel, Bruno and Anshel, have in common that they had been writers in the face of the Holocaust, and that, through their persistence, they resisted the obliteration of the individual which the Nazis worked for. In Grossman's fantasy, neither

Bruno nor Anshel could be killed. They both live on, beyond Nazism, to continue telling their tales, through language invented and created, archaic and new, from the past to the present.

In the third section, the first person narrator, now Momik himself, accompanies Anshel Wasserman back to 'there', that is, to the camp where Wasserman was incarcerated, and the text now bears witness to the attempts to exterminate him, as specifically ordered and also attempted by Herr Neigel, the commandant, himself. But the failure of the attempt leads to a dance of sick humour and to the reprise of the Sheherezade theme. Herr Neigel becomes dependent on the stories to be told by Wasserman, who has it within his power to withhold them. After all, those stories are his most intimate possession, and they belong exclusively to him, as they are exclusively under his control. As Herr Neigel recalls his own childhood attachments and the part played in them by Wasserman's stories, which were published in German, he needs and wants the author more and more. And this happens as less and less does that author have any desire to cling to life. Herr Neigel yearns for these childhood stories, only now he insists on stories to be created for him alone. The paradox here is that the stories written by Wasserman were stories of adventure and miraculous redemption, where good unexpectedly triumphed over evil, and where the good guys intervened to save those in distress at the hands of their cruel tormentors. The deal to save his life is first rejected by Wasserman, as, in contrast to Sheherezade, he is not only indifferent to life, but actively wants to die. The new deal now though, reluctantly accepted, is that Wasserman should tell his own, new stories, and, if they appeal to Neigel, he will try to kill him as a special favour. If not, Wasserman will be condemned to live on. In an odd twist, Anshel invites Neigel to join him in the composition of his ad hoc plots, thus adapting the notion of reader response to one of cooperation between Nazi and Jew. Realism can extend no further, so rather than move the story on to a rounded conclusion, we come to the final section so far removed from sequential plot, to Kazik's encyclopaedia.

Writing about Writing the Holocaust

Grossman not only writes about the Holocaust, obsessively so, in *See Under: Love*. He also constantly interposes himself as a witness and a character in the fiction, commentating on his own efforts to write up the subject. In fact, the Grossman narrator/hero is a constant presence in the oeuvre in a combination of variations. Two anchors lock the extensive output in position, first, the standpoint of the child, the pre-adolescent who moves, adjacent to the adult world, and about to enter it, and second, the unpredictable as well as jagged movement of the principal character/narrator. This lends particular relevance to the title of one of his books, *The Zigzag Kid*. Such a 'kid' does not fit into regular and consistent frameworks, such as squares or circles, and keeps going off in contrary directions. Thus, the dual positioning of the narrator as outsider and insider, as one who witnesses and inscribes the event, as well as participating in it. The nature of the typical Grossman narrative is also of two shades, naturalistic and fantastic. The larger picture of the overall oeuvre too is dual, consisting of both reportage and magic realism in the fiction, sometimes in combination.

This work, presumed to be aimed primarily at the child reader, presents a child hero, aware of his orphaned state, but determined to enter the late father's sphere, that of policing. Much of Grossman's work indeed is situated on the border between legitimate and forbidden activity, and this motif is repeated in *Mishehu laruts ito* (*Someone to Run With*). The age of the child in *The Zigzag*

Kid, thirteen, is also of the nature of borderlands, on the frontier of adulthood (the bar-mitzvah). It transpires in the story that the one who initiates the hero into the life of robbery and fantasy, Felix Glick, is not only a notorious international criminal, hunted and eventually captured through the agency of the detective father, but is also his grandfather, the father of his deceased mother. So, our 'hero' is the issue of a criminal line, a product of a union between criminal and policeman.

The blurred boundary in Grossman's work between (auto)biography and fiction is illustrated by the long work, *Sefer hadiqduq hapnimi* (1991, *The Book of Intimate Grammar*, 1994). This follows the young Aron over four years of his young life, anticipating his *bar mitzvah* at the opening of the book, growing up in Beit Hakerem, Jerusalem, in the 60s. Although adopting the third person narrative mode, it has the feel of a story about the author himself, as it reflects, as does *See Under: Love*, such an expression of private thoughts and feelings, also running perhaps fairly much in parallel to the currents of the author's own life. But again the stories regaled are very much concerned with other people, and the need for the young chief protagonist to make his discovery of the actual events of their lives, past and present. All this involves an effort of interpretation, the dismantling of secret signs and symbols, and the translation of the objects of the adult world into child language. This is the 'internal grammar' of the title, where the 'other' is shunted, interpreted and retold, into an inner language. Awakening curiosity and progress towards adult style enlightenment accompany burgeoning sexuality and obsession with the girls of his world. This is all part of his learning mode.

The typical Grossman story is set in another land of 'there', where the 'there' represents that remote region which everyone, of necessity, must know deep down, as it is the world of childhood. This world is a venue of insatiable curiosity and discovery, the world where the child must grow up following a learning process and loss of innocence. It is a world full of adventures, that of the picaresque, where the hero is also the villain. It is also a world of the *Bildungsroman*, where the child learns to be an adult, something that also cannot be avoided. It is this adult but mysterious region that the author, now become narrator, has to discover, that nether and sinister cave of imagination, where the evil impulses are turned into gruesome reality, most absolutely, in the Holocaust. That dark passage of history had in actual history little light shining in, and the space for heroic action was constricted in relation to the weight of overwhelming evil. So Grossman has recreated his two literary heroes in *See Under: Love*. They are Schulz and Wasserman, who, in the experimental novel, persisted in their fictional fight, and held out. Wasserman could not die, and Schulz plunges into the sea.

In the struggle between the dominator and the dominated, the apparent imbalance may be corrected by the notion of mutual dependence. What may seem to be victory can turn out to be another kind of defeat, and what had been defeat or death can be washed or written away. This world is an ongoing zigzag of constantly changing fortunes; the apparent force of the iron fist may well crack itself. What appears to be absolute freedom achieved through total domination can also constitute objective enslavement, as the oppressor is then dependent on the victim for his own existence. Grossman's writing concerns itself with this dialogue between two opposing forces, and is built up of a patchwork of antitheses; child-adult, here-there, fact-fiction, Nazi-Jew, Israeli-Arab, policeman-criminal. And sometimes then, their roles might be reversed. So much of Grossman's work sounds like autobiography. But this is misleading as far as external factuality is concerned. Rather, the outer has become the inner, and the two intertwined. This creates the internal grammar.

VI

BIOGRAPHY AND THE STORY:
JERZY KOSINSKI (1933-1991)

Very few authors have faced as radical a challenge on almost every front as has Kosinski, whose reputation suffered so much in his later years, and which went into a further decline following his death. It is surely timely that a further reassessment be conducted, as well as an attempt at forming an objective view of the facts of his unusual and highly eventful career.[1]

Background

Jerzy Kosinski was attacked for depicting Poles as anti-Semitic and primitive in *The Painted Bird*, from which the accepted account of his life is taken. Questions were also raised over the

---

[1] For a list of Kosinski's books, see bibliography.
Under pen-name of Joseph Novak:
The Future is Ours, Comrade (1960).
No Third Path (1962).

authenticity and truth of the picture there presented.[2] But most of the facts are agreed anyway. He was born in Lodz on June 14, 1943 to the Jewish couple, Moses and Elzbieta Lewinkopf,[3] and lived through the Holocaust in Poland, when he was placed by his parents, (who changed the family name to Kosinski to make it sound more Polish), in the care of a peasant woman, who died soon afterwards. According to the account contained in the book, which seems at least partially autobiographical, he roamed alone in the Polish countryside. The climax of misfortune hits him when he was eventually thrown into a cesspool, from which he could not emerge for quite some time, following which incident, he lost the power of speech. After the war, he was found by his parents, and he regained his speech after suffering the shock of a skiing accident. He studied in Lomonosov University in the USSR, but fled to New York in December 1957, arriving on the 20th of the month.[4] In his own words: 'I left behind being an inner *emigré* trapped in spiritual exile. America was to give shelter to my real self and I wanted to become its writer-in-residence.'[5] Two years later, he began writing non-fiction on collective society. In New York, he studied both History and Political Science, receiving MAs in both. He then enrolled as a doctoral student at Columbia University. His writing career was initiated with studies of the Communist system, under the pseudonym of Joseph Novak,[6] before

---

[2] See particularly James Park Sloane, *Jerzy Kosinski: A Biography* (New York: Dutton, 1996). See also the article on Kosinski in the *Village Voice* of June 1982. In Lavers' account (see below), he is described as being of 'Jewish ancestry'.

[3] See David Patterson, Alan L. Berger and Sarita Cargas (eds.) *Encyclopaedia of Holocaust Literature* (Westport Ct.: Oryx Press, 2002).

[4] For another version of this account, transcribed directly from Kosinski himself in telephone calls, see Norman Lavers, *Jerzy Kosinski* (New York: Bantam Books, 1982).

[5] See appendix in *Cockpit* (London: Arrow Books, 1982).

[6] See bibliographical note above.

completing his first novel, *The Painted Bird*, in 1965. Following the publication of his second novel, *Steps*, in 1968, which met with huge international success, he taught English Literature at Princeton University (1969-1970), and, in the following year was appointed Professor of Dramatic Prose and Criticism at the Yale University School of Drama. He was accused of fabrication and plagiarism, as well as of heavy use of non-attributed editors, but no charge was ever confirmed or accepted by Kosinski himself. The highly successful novel, *Being There*, however, seemed to be based on the earlier Polish bestseller, *The Career of Nikodem Dyzma*, and his reputation suffered in later years. He died in New York, in 1991, when he was found suffocated, with a plastic bag round his head.

Kosinski published exclusively in English, and served as an academic as well as an author, as professor of English at Yale University amongst other major institutions. He began his writing career as a commentator on the collectivisation programme in the USSR. His final writings were published posthumously under the title of *Passing By* (1992). He also wrote screen plays, such as *Being There*, based on his own novel of that name. He won many national awards, and was also a screen actor, playing the part of Zinoviev in *Reds*, for example.

The Painted Bird

The Painted Bird is Kosinski's first novel, and it seems (as with everything in the author's career, the borderline between autobiography and fiction is very finely drawn) to serve as a template for his overall opus. Critics have described it as 'semi-autobiographical', and Elie Wiesel has called it a chronicle in the *New York Times Book Review*. Kosinski argued that it was true to the basic experience of Jewish children under the Nazis. It is related in the first person, opening with an account of a boy, who is only six years old at the start of the narrative, which coincides with the outbreak of the Second World War. But it is introduced in the third person, and when we get to the narrative, much remains untold. Perhaps the narrator himself is unsure of his own status, as he has been let go by his parents into a threatening world, set to survive the German occupation as best he can. He knows he is an outcast, marked for extermination, possibly Jew, possibly Gipsy. His swarthy features are a giveaway, and he is constantly expecting betrayal, affront and assault. We are not told the name of the region where he finds himself, nor even his name. Perhaps, as a child, he does not know any of these things for certain, although many other external facts are presented to the reader as part of that history. Presumably, he is in a region of Eastern Poland, now occupied by the Nazis, following the *Blitzkrieg* of September 1939. So we are immediately introduced to one of the central issues of Kosinski's work; the fluidity of the parameters, the uncertainty in the mind of the reader as to what extent the material presented is documentary, in this case a memoir, and to what extent, this is the product of his imagination. The events are horrific, the environment barbaric, gripped by superstition, perversion, cruelty and sadism.

Seemingly, the novel is based on his own life story. He is handed over to a foster mother for the purpose of survival. But she soon dies, and he has to wander round the villages, offering his labour. All only seek to exploit him, and are willing to turn him over without any qualms. The horrors that he observes from his various hidden positions in barns or at inconspicuous corners are unbearable to contemplate, let alone experience. But, even as a desperately deprived child, he finds that he has a mission. When he observes the miller plucking out the eyes of a ploughman in a fit of jealousy over his wife, the child observes: 'I made a promise to myself to remember everything I saw; if someone should pluck out my eyes, then I would retain the memory of all that I had seen for as long as I lived.' (44) The child's function is now signed up as witness, and much of Kosinski's writing can now be understood in this way. The image of the painted bird also assumes a central place. The peasant Lekh paints a selected bird, one of the many that he adopts, and sets it free. This bird tries to 'convince' other birds of its own species that it is one of them. But it is pecked to death. Perhaps this can be said to parallel the narrator's own life story, his attempts to survive, to present normality, to seek acceptability, and, ultimately, to fail.

The novel is one of memory and record. We recognise much of the known history, and the boy's story moves on through time. The partisan resistance is strengthened. The Winter of 1944 is harsh. He has already noted that the trains are being used for unusual purposes, and he can now observe the transports with the masses of Jews being inhumanly taken to their deaths. Noted too is the reaction of the peasants, gloating over what they see as just punishment, meted out to a despised race for the crucifixion carried out by the ancestors. The child is also aware of his own ambivalent nature. His contact with German officers leads him to worship this apparently magnificent species of mankind, so superior to himself. They are the picture of perfection, in their splendid uniforms. One officer, for example: '[s]eemed an example of neat perfection that could not be sullied; the smooth, polished skin of his face, the bright golden hair showing under his peaked cap, his pure metal eyes.' (110) This constitutes a formidable combination of something inhuman, perhaps superhuman (metal) and infallibility. It also leads him to be doubly ashamed of his own appearance: 'I thought how good it would be to have such a gleaming and hairless skull instead of my Gipsy face which was so feared and disliked by decent people.' (110)

The child though is saved, by a priest, who hands him over to one Gabos, who beats him mercilessly, savagely and regularly, almost to the point of extinction. Horrors seem to have no end, and, when he drops a missal (he had been appointed altar boy), he is cast into a pit of manure. This experience removes his power of speech, and he is rendered dumb (until two years later, when speech is restored after the shock of a skiing accident). The war proceeds, and, if the Poles and the Germans had not been bad enough, we now have the even more savage Kalmuks, who carry out the most savage pogroms imaginable, sadistic mass rapes and slaughter. But the Soviets then take over, offering salvation to the child, who so enthusiastically embraces their doctrines. After the war's end, his parents miraculously and inexplicably turn up, although by that point, he only wants independence in the sort of brave new world offered by the Soviets. The novel concludes with the recovery of the power of speech, and the prospect of uncertain future. This is the first narrative account of the author's perplexing and troubled life.

Steps

Steps continues in the vein of his earlier novel, deploying the first person narrator, together with an oblique reference to some of the facts of the external world. Similarly, much of the motivation of the central character is shrouded in mystery, and the sequence of events seems puzzling. We are presented with a sequence of apparently unconnected episodes, related in the first person. The motifs are governed by erotic desire and sexual activity, domination and torture. There is much concern with mirroring, seeing himself both from within, his own perspective, and from without, as in a mirror, or as seen by another. The novel opens with a brief account of himself, a visitor to a village, who invites a girl, previously unknown to him, to join him in his travels and in the big city, where he will care for all her needs. A flashback introduces a different scene at a beach, then later, a sanatorium where he is employed as a skiing instructor. But then, there are scenes in sanatoria and in the army. We have the random associations of the surrealist, with the linkage established by mood, with the narrator as victim. But sometimes, he is a highly privileged victim. Victim can become judge and executioner (44). The basic form is a memoir, with recall of peasant life, and then association with the Communist Party.

The 'steps' that the narrator takes are sometimes those that proceed from his status of victim to that of executioner. If he is wronged, he learns to exact secret revenge, 'secret', because that is the most assured path to success, working behind the scenes. The Kosinger hero works in the dark, and his identity is clouded, perhaps transformed, certainly unknown to others. The thing that is enjoyed is erotic pleasure, pushed to the limits, but conducted anonymously. Indeed, hardly anyone has a name, certainly not the object of desire, and nor himself. There is also not much of a divide between the erotic and the sadistic. He stretches the imagination to encompass the horrific, and he can come to terms with the ultimate in rampant cruelty by lowering the tone to a level of factuality. In a conversation conducted about an architect who designs, amongst other things, a concentration camp, he paraphrases his concerns for its appropriate design thus: 'Above all, it had to be functional.' (63) This was his guiding doctrine. And how justify the procedure? In the sense that one likes animals, but recognises that rats (which are also animals of course) have to be exterminated: 'It's a problem of hygiene. Rats have to be removed.' (64)

This strangely constructed and conceived novel implicitly reviews the narrator's life, one in which, initially through circumstances forced on him, and then through choice and adoption of the survival option, it is extremity that is proposed. His history consists of confrontation with Nazis and Communists, and the avoidance of the consequences of both. There are controllers, perpetrators and victims. In a related episode of a caged woman, he learns to understand those who tolerated, and perhaps even initiated the situation. In a discussion of murder, the jury could understand, that is, enter the skin of, the murderer, but not of the victim (95). And, after his own emigration, he gets involved in a nasty protection racket.

How can we understand the narrator's problematic identity? That seems to follow from his life story. He had initially survived by adopting an alternative identity, from a very early age, six years old. Perhaps he pursued that line by becoming an emigrant (in itself, a life change), and English language writer (covering up his initial language), and the anonymous and mysterious figure behind his narratives. He writes: 'If I could magically speak their language and change the shade of my skin, the shape of my skull, the texture of my hair, I would transform myself into one of them. This way I would drive away from me the image of what I had once been and what I might become...This change would give me no other choice but to remain alive.' (134-5) Just as the choice is between life and death, so the means of achieving that desideratum, and of arriving at some sort of equilibrium, seems to be the selection, on the part of the author, of either the original self or of some other.

Being There

In some ways, *Being There* is Kosinski's most famous book, partly due to the success of the film mad of the book, starring Peter Sellers in his last role. However, it is also a problematic piece in regard to its status and the question of its use of an unattributed Polish source.[7] But it seems that rather than plagiarising the Polish source, Kosinski is citing it in order to point up the differences and contrast between Dyzma, the Polish figure in the earlier novel, who is crude and cunning, and Chance, who lacks will and any purpose whatever. Regarded as a self-standing work, *Being There* is not only exciting and beautifully executed, but also highly illuminating in the light that it casts over the author's opus as a whole, and over the author behind it. The book is economically written, and treats one issue exclusively, never sidetracked.

The central character is in a sense not a person at all. He is known by the name of Chance, to indicate the manner in which he happened on the household in which he found himself, protected by an anonymous 'old man'. Chance works in the garden, which he makes his sole interest in life. He has no family, and apparently no background or history. His mind is a blank. He can use language, but only very mechanically, and he has no capacity for abstract thought. He cannot read or write, knows no one, and has no contact with the world beyond his own domain. He loves television, because, by turning on and off and changing channels, he can control the switches and the shape of the material, which he then imitates in his own speech and gestures. There is no external corroboration of even his bare existence.

---

[7] The novel most often quoted as the basis for Kosinski's book is the Polish work, *The Career of Nikodem Dyzma* by Tadeusz Dolega-Mostowicz, published in 1932, a work enormously popular in its time, and so certainly known to Kosinski.

The plot is set in motion by the death of the old man. The estate passes into other hands, and those responsible now let him go. In the world beyond, he is totally helpless, and on his venture out, he is knocked down by a car, and his leg crushed. Taken in by the chauffeur and the lady in charge, Mrs. Benjamin Rand, wife of a highly influential magnate, he is housed in magnificent surroundings, and cared for. As no one knows who he is, and he can provide no further information, all his statements are interpreted as nuggets of laconic wisdom. When he says that he is a gardener, this is taken to mean that his name is Gardiner, and from then on, he is known as Chauncey Gardiner. His talk of gardens is understood to be metaphorical, standing in for his grasp of the way that the world works, requiring nurture and attention to the health of its roots. In a context devoid of real hope and understanding, where the country, i.e. the USA, seems to be veering out of control, with soaring unemployment and a catastrophic economic situation, Chance's gnomic responses to questions seem to hold out hope for an eventual remedy. Rand introduces him to the President, who is duly impressed with his assessment of the situation: ' "All will be well as long as the roots aren't severed." ' This sounds like true wisdom, and more, seems also to indicate the light at the end of the tunnel. The fact that he has been taken up by Rand, and then by the President himself, makes an enormous impression on the public at large, apparently thirsty for such doctrine. But all Chance's responses are taken either from his experience tending the garden of the house in which he lived, or are based on imitations of television gestures. But the President quotes his words in an important televised speech, and he is then described as '[o]ne of the chief architects of the President's policy speech.' (84) Someone says of him: ' "Mr. Gardiner has the uncanny ability of reducing complex matters to the simplest of human terms." ' (106)

Of course, behind all this is one who is scarcely a person at all. He does not even seem to possess sexual desire, only indulging in the passive function of watching (Scopophilia). The Agencies try to dig up information about him, without success of course, as there is nothing to dig up. He remains 'a blank page', both for the Soviets and for the Americans. This brief novel concludes with Chance back in a garden, trying to resume his familiar routine, rejecting the glories and temptations of the world: 'Not a thought lifted itself from Chance's brain. Peace filled his chest.'

Our hero is a blank, but he is invested with all the imaginings and desires of a hungry populace. He is a necessary projection, and no more fitting container can be found for such needs than an empty vessel. That is an ideal. Can this indeed be regarded as a portrayal of Kosinski himself? A character without a record, an empty space to be filled? The little boy hero of *The Painted Bird* had to reject his identity in order to survive. *Steps* tells of the next stage in a shifting kaleidoscope of scenarios. *Being There* empties out the container totally, and can be filled with the content provided by any reader, taking on the character of what is desired, like the manna in the desert for the Children of Israel.

The Devil Tree

The novelist adopts the technique of shifting from first to third person, allowing a view of the character both from within and without, in a laconic and distilled style. As in his earlier work, he is primarily concerned with extreme violence. The character of Jonathan Whelan, a person who seems to be a tramp living in New York, is also puzzlingly rich. We discover that he is an opium smoker, and had been a dropout in Burma, with his beloved Karen. Typically, and as manifest in his fiction generally, he appears as a split personality, a fact that he himself recognises. He seeks to suppress the child in himself, as he is determined not to appear helpless. On the one hand, he is a screaming child, but, on the other, he seeks self-control.

Violence, as it is manifest in the novel, imposes its terrifying grip on the principal protagonist from childhood. In response, he becomes an exemplary 'tough guy', deeply sceptical of himself: 'I have always suspected everyone who likes me of having poor judgment. I despise them for being so easily taken in.'(59) There is the dark pervasive presence of random, causeless massacres, as relayed by the character, Richard. His own sex drive is enormous, matching the insatiable needs of Karen, who, unlike him, is unable to achieve satisfaction. This, together with his obsession with death and the paths leading to it, constitutes the principal motif of the work. This, like other works of Kosinski, is a story of primal urges, on the one hand, and the effort to bring them under control, on the other. Impulse and analysis constitute the narrative, as is explicated in his account of an encounter group. Within that framework, one person, a history teacher, says that: 'Only someone of my background…could act out a tragedy one minute and a burlesque the next. She said that I would never really let go, that I would always resist my impulses and remain detached.'(95)

The novel consists of monologues on the part of Whalen, together with addresses made to him, and descriptions of himself viewed from the outside. Much of that character was apparently formed by his dominating millionaire father, Sumner Whalen. Jonathan tries to influence his company in a humanitarian direction, but his own end is implicit disaster. We see him walking towards the lake in Geneva, following the refusal of the doctors at the clinic where he is being treated, to allow him any insight into his own condition. The mists of the lake allude to the dimness of his future, and the closure of the novel parallels that of the central character's life.

Cockpit

In another of the series of autobiographical fictions (to describe the mix of literal self-portraiture and fiction that the author adopts), *Cockpit* presents another alternative identity in the person of Tarden. Characteristically, Tarden is an employee in the Secret Service of his country, a container that not only allows for the creation of a new identity, but that actively demands it. Like the other novels, *Cockpit* is episodic, composed of sometimes discrete sections, and the book as a whole is otherwise a continuous narrative, not divided into separate chapters. Also characteristically, for someone on the margins of society, his favourite activity is observation rather than participation, looking at all individuals for their behaviour patterns and deriving sexual excitement from this more than from actual practice. It is in this book that he goes into the details of his defection, an extremely elaborate and sophisticated process, requiring senior status, considerable patience, and much ingenuity. Following, his natural bent, he is then recruited to the American Secret Service. But this is by no means a sympathetic hagiography. On the contrary, we have a self-portrait of a sexual predator and ruthless murderer, the latter seemingly an inclination lodged in him from infancy. He constantly engages in mental and physical exercises in order to test and extend his competence. He notes his own lack of emotional response to scenes of destruction and suffering, adding: 'Perhaps the explanations for my behaviour, if there are any, are rooted in an area of my past to which I have no access.' (121) He describes his own sadistic acts in great detail, including how he brings harm to families and animals unknown.

He concludes with a sickeningly gruesome and possibly realistic portrait of the aged in Florida, an imagined dreamland for the retired. But this is of course also a product of his own aging despair.

It may not be fruitful to speculate on what proportion of the novels relates literally to the author's own life and experiences. According to the biographers,[8] he gives contradictory answers to the question posed, of whether the accounts are facts or fiction. When challenged about fact, he may argue that he is writing fiction, and that he is therefore not bound to adhere to the actual and literal lines of the events. But when it is then said that these are fictions, he may then argue that all that appears in his work is true. These accounts can be reconciled. Whilst the narrative is invented in the detail of the names and the events, it is apparently all derived, inevitably, from his own experience, and thus does correspond with aspects of his own mind, imagination, and psychological reach. He has also claimed that this is the normal practice of the creative writer.

Blind Dates and Passion

Kosinski continued to build his fictions in the manner he had established, episodically, layered in plotted sequences, integrating fragments of life history. *Blind Date*[9] tells of one George Levanter, whose biography bears a remarkably close resemblance to the author's own. But how close this is, and whether the biographical element is adjudged to assess the material as Kosinski's own story, we cannot tell. Also, not whether this be the central issue. Levanter is in Switzerland on a skiing resort, and then incidentally we learn

---

[8] See for example Lavers, op. cit.
[9] *Blind Date* (Boston: Houghton Mifflin Company, 1977).

of his earlier life in Eastern Europe, when he had been the lover of his own mother. This Levanter had emigrated, building up a profile for this purpose with great difficulty, initiating a career as a photographer of considerable technical originality. He is also a man of massive and perverted passion, learning how to perform rape, including the ability to carry out such a monstrous practice unseen by the victim, the so-called 'blind date'.

This character then seems to be a projection of the author's own person and story. He even includes episodes well known to the general public such as the horrific Sharon Tate massacre in California. We have extremes of action; violence, sex, stories of repression, his known political stance, and his own position on a range of issues. George Levanter's life seems to consist of a succession of such blind dates, and the novel which contains an account of some of them over this period in his life acts as a further numbered volume in this rather strange form of human comedy.

Kosinski adopts the name Fabian for the central character of his novel, *Passion Play*.[10] But Fabian shares many of the personal and professional marks of all the central figures of Kosinski's novels. He loves active sport, and here, he is a professional and very successful polo player. He seems too to be in sequence with earlier works, noticing in himself the signs of aging. He is a constant observer of human behaviour, and a persistent mischief-maker. He is also a sexual predator. He notes however, that this is a uniquely human trait, as man is the only mammal that can turn up his own erotic heat at will. His life lies on the fringes of society, both in the jet set and in the *demi monde* of illicit adventure. Fabian reveals that his inordinate ambition derives from a fear of decline into failure and decrepitude. He has to fight hard in order to achieve a unique

---

[10] Jerzy Kosinski, *Passion Play* (New York: St. Martin's Press, 1979).

place. As a polo player and rider (his single talent), he works against the grain, not together with the team, but striving for his own excellence, competing not against the other team, or indeed, against other individuals, but rather against himself, and against the standards that he himself sets up. Polo is, for him and for his associates, the most competitive of sports, and the ultimate testing ground of endurance and determination. Fabian is the man to be set in this context, both for the game itself, and, incidentally, for the rest of what remains in life.

Typically, the novel includes descriptions of extreme violence, perverse sexuality, and even self-mutilation. This is the 'passion play'. The focus of consciousness, Fabian, bears these messages, not understanding the springs of his own motivation until the consequences of such impulses are realised in action. But they are always on the edge of experience: 'To Fabian, the intensity of his acts was always knowable; and he seldom had a comparable knowledge of his motive.' (61) After the event comes the reflection and analysis. Through this existentialist drive, he discovers himself through what he does, and not the other way about. This is his existence, that which determines who he is.

Another theme running through this novel, as in many others of Kosinski's works is the proximity to the sources of external power, here played out in Latin America. Political control goes hand in hand with sexual fantasy and fulfilment, just as competitive sport at its most testing edges is also erotic. As Fabian observes later, in another context, the characters seek a position 'between desire and gratification'. Fantasy finds ultimate freedom in transexuality, the ability to enjoy the sexual contact of both partners in one. In an excursus into Fabian's background, the author tells us of the tough childhood he had endured, raised by a foster father, and always held as an outsider, who had to harden himself in order to survive. This is a reprise of the themes of the early novels; the child in disguise, growing a hide of protection in the life of the village, and given the most sordid tasks to earn the right to stay alive. The past merges with the present, and shapes its contours. The hero's determining characteristic is that of an outcast, someone on the fringes of the society in which he is reared. As such, he can instinctively sense the degree of outsider strain in others, as with the woman Stella, who he knows is black, although she appears to be entirely white. It turns out that she was born white to black parents, who then felt that they had to turn out onto the world, and seek here future as a white person in white society. Evidently, this did not entirely succeed, and her sense of exclusion persisted, until her meeting up with Fabian, a similar case of displacement. Now, imagination has to take over, '...a prodigality of images'. (210)

Fabian's concern is to be free, which means, in his sense, to determine his own fate. He turns down an unconditional financial gift from his beloved Vanessa, who is a generation younger than himself. He leaves her to allow himself the necessary space, and also to give her the chance to make herself, in his words: 'To give her the right to confront her life on her own, he had to unfasten the chain that bound her to him.' (269) He had to free himself from her, as, for her, passion was no longer play. The novel concludes, that he has to remain '[i]n combat with an enemy only he could see.' He has to continue to fight, which, for him, is to be, and to achieve that alone.

The final phase of his fiction

Pinball[11] is one of his last novels, and constitutes what seems to be a thinly veiled statement about his own life and situation. The central character is Patrick Domostroy, a once great composer now working in a pinball joint in New York. There are various elements manifestly in common with Kosinski's own life, the fact that Domostroy is originally from 'Eastern Europe', but more importantly that he has been alleged not to have composed his music single handed. Since one of the principal charges made against Kosinski himself is that he had received substantial editorial assistance in the writing of his books, even verging on ghost writing, it looks here as though Domostroy could easily be a projection of the author's own situation, making the shift from literature to music. In the prime of life, Domostroy had lost the will to compose, and the question posed is: what went wrong? The other major figure in the novel is a hidden presence, that of the rock music genius, Goddard, pursued avidly by his fans, and particularly by the lovely Andrea, who enlists Domostroy in her search in return for financial support as well as sexual gratification.

Pinball is a kind of detective story, in which we have to discover where and who is Goddard. In a manner that is now familiar in the Kosinski narrative, the reader is taken through to the ultimate of an obsession, but, on the way, he/she is also dealt multiple hints in thematic bumps. Much concern is evinced with the notion of paraphrasing, here deflected into music, but with parallels noted with literature, that is, themes stated by one creator, and then adapted by someone else, maybe transcribed for another instrument. In literature too, this has been practised constantly, sometimes acknowledged, and more often, not. Kosinski too carried out

---

[11] Jerzy Kosinski, *Pinball* (London: Arrow Books, 1983; first pub. 1982).

this practice. The other notable Kosinski theme is that of hiding, leading to multiple identity. Goddard, whom we soon encounter in the text and along the narrative, strives for anonymity, and yet he ascribes to Domostroy the soubriquet of Jekyll and Hyde. In fact, both of the leading protagonists are hiding, and are used to stripping off veils, and substituting alternatives. Here are two musicians, describing circles around each other. They in fact meet regularly, although Domostroy, at first, does not identify the hidden Goddard. Identity, disguise, search for freedom, the interplay between the dominator and the dominated; these are the motifs that the narrative first establishes and then takes the reader through in a progression of episodes and stills. Goddard /Osten (his alter ego) is determined to trace the photographer behind the photographs being sent to him, through the black and beautiful pianist, Donna. The chase achieves a bloody climax, with the identities disclosed. Domostroy and Osten however remain alive, the former unable to separate life from art in the way that Goddard has managed. Domostroy ends up uncertain, with nowhere to go.

A Very Particular Approach

Kosinski was concerned with the question of how to write and of what constitutes the practice of literature. A collection of his occasional essays and published *obiter dicta* and speeches was published posthumously, in which this theme was constantly touched upon.[12] He quotes his old friend, Mr. André Wat, who is said to have told him: ' "Write a book that is most innocent and

---

[12] Jerzy Kosinski, *Passing By: Selected Essays, 1962-1991* (New York: Random House, 1992; Paperback ed. New York: Grove Press, 1995). The author did not have a chance to overview the final version, which was brought to press by his widow, Mrs. Jerzy (Kiki) Kosinski.

most depraved at the same time. Most innocent, because it will be about a child – about yourself or me – but do it in sexual terms so that it is stirring; it is the only thing that makes a stir. Take a stand outside that process and try not to be alienated from it but, rather, be its presence and its absence at the same time – that is how the creative process happens." [13] This is in fact what the author aspires to, and it probably serves as his guiding mantra. In his books, he tries to be both present and absent; present, because that is what lends his writing such dangerous spark and reality, but absent too, so that he may preserve the objective view. The Kosinski figure (the narrator or central character, the focus of consciousness), stands both within the action and outside, leading the reader to become unsure of his own bearings, and lose too the sense of historical actuality.[14] Kosinski can excuse any deviation from the description of the literal event by arguing that he is not necessarily interested in explicit memory, but rather in the use of that past, as summoned up, in the metaphors created. There would in fact be no point in merely reprising an event that had already occurred. This adopted practice he names 'autofiction', presenting what is indeed true, but true in the larger sense that '[b]ooks are democratic in that they grant readers the freedom to interpret their meaning.'[15] He goes on to argue of his own stance, shared with that of Mr. Wat, in addressing the reader: 'I am your entrance into yourself and into history at the same time.' Thus the author's work points both inwards and outwards simultaneously. It is notoriously difficult to pin this work down as though it were historiography. It

---

[13] Op. cit., 4.

[14] The issue of actuality and historical truth, publicly mooted by the article in the *Village Voice*, is raised again in vivid dramatic terms by the play *More Lies About Jerzy* by Davey Holmes, performed at the New End theatre, Hampstead, in November 2002.

[15] Op. cit., 21.

is both more and less; certainly different. As a child in the Second World War, he has learnt a particular lesson in the absorption of that material into his oeuvre: 'Dramatic! Traumatic! Dramatic! That is exactly it! To turn trauma into drama, to show Auschwitz as the fullness of life.'[16] What he tells may or may not have happened to him in the historical sense. But it certainly constitutes a truth, perhaps of another sort. It is a truth of the period, and thus an accurate portrayal of the human condition. It is this that remains the source of its power, and the way that it reaches out to the readership. The Kosinski protagonist is typically, according to a critic of his work, a caged bird.[17] This central image in the writing premises a paradox, that of the cage pre-existing the bird, and needing its presence. However, in some cases, the bird can exit the cage, as was the case with the author's own experience in leaving Eastern Europe.

We cannot ignore the fact that it may well be the borderline between 'auto-fiction' and factuality that lies at the root of the fascination exerted. This does not resolve the question raised by forked approach, but indeed raises further questions. Kosinski is clearly aware of this, and tantalises us ever more. He writes: 'In a way, all my novels are confessional, confessing to the reader the sins of the protagonist – and *maybe* of the author. They are also non judgmental, morally open ended, they encourage the reader to judge what, to him or her, is right or wrong.'[18] So we do not necessarily know whether what is written relates literally to the author, to the events of history, or whether they are the narrative (and fictional) creation of the writer, who nevertheless asserts their metaphysical truth. Kosinski also most vehemently rejects the charge

[16] Op. cit., 35.
[17] Paul Lilly, *Words in Search of Victims: The Achievement of Jerzy Kosinski* (Kent: The Kent State University Press, 1988), 1 and c.
[18] See *Passing By*, 162.

that his first works exaggerate the nature of the events of that horrific period of his life. Soon after the appearance of his first and groundbreaking work, in Switzerland 1963, he asserted: '[h]aving spent my childhood and adolescence during the war and post-war years in Eastern Europe, I know that real events had been more brutal than the most bizarre fantasies.'[19] So, whilst there may be uncertainties in regard to the authenticity of his personal record in regard to the literal biographical material, there can be no dispute on the larger matter of the general truth. People are not only capable of behaving in the manner portrayed; in fact, they actually did behave in that way. In support of his argument, the author quotes documentary sources, as articulated by those who witnessed and experienced the horrendous events of the period, and so felt at first hand what was committed. He began his writing career as a straight reporter, conveying from within the feel of ordinary life as lived in the USSR. His first book[20] is a piece of reportage, conducted with the aid of his privileged position: 'As a minor bureaucrat from one of the satellite countries, enjoying the confidence of a number of highly situated USSR officials who were responsible for my visit, I was invited to Russia for a protracted stay and allowed to arrange my Soviet life according to my own wishes, without being hampered or limited by anyone.' (15) It is in this first, non fictional work that Kosinski conceives of the concept, the 'cage', in order to categorise a life. One of his chapters bears that heading, in a description of personal and family life, where private matters become public. It is here too, in an assessment of the post-Nazi situation, that he notes the prevalence of a vicious anti-Semitism. But we also may note that the transition from documentary reportage to the sort of 'fiction' that he projects is virtually

---

[19] Op. cit., 184.
[20] Novak, Joseph, *The Future is Ours, Comrade* (London: The Bodley Head, 1960).

seamless and unremarkable. It can be seen be seen as part of a continuum, a continuum that can not be easily divided into the separate boxes of documentary/autobiography, on the one hand, and fiction, on the other. He had begun his writing in the first mode, but then opened his imagination out to the freer and less inhibiting genre of fiction. It is within this framework that the author developed the unique amalgam, the remarkable 'autofiction', that remains at once maddening and entrancing, if just for the fact of being on that borderline. But, even without complete and satisfactory labelling that would allow for categorisation, the Kosinski fictional opus does remain unique and compelling, constituted of a series of works not matched for authority, terror, compactness and grip.

VII

TELLING IT AS IT IS: PRIMO LEVI

What is Man?

No writer has succeeded in capturing the public imagination as the very exemplar of Holocaust survival and representation as much as the Italian Primo Levi (1919-1987). This may be considered surprising as it took many years Levi's writing to be accepted. Not that, as is so often claimed, Levi did not pen his reactions until many years had passed after the experience. As we see from the various dates of the publication of his classic work on Auschwitz, he composed it soon after the war's end. But the book sank almost into oblivion, and it was only when many years had passed that *If This is a Man*[1] became recognised as a classic, and now has iconic status.[2]

His life history is that as a young man and trained chemist from Turin, he had joined a partisan band to fight the Fascists. He was captured and sent to a detention camp in Fossoli, near Modena, after the German invasion of Italy. On the 21 February 1944, the Jews were detached from the rest of the group and despatched to Auschwitz. At that time, the general population in Italy had very little notion of the exact nature of the war being fought, and Levi had believed that his status as a partisan had more significance for the enemy than the (for him) rather marginal issue that he happened to be Jewish. He also did not realise at that stage what the reality of Auschwitz really consisted of. As it turned out, of the 125 men sent to the camp on his particular convoy, only three, including himself, managed to return to Italy in the wake of the liberation. The two accounts, *If This is a Man* and *The Truce*, are the first literary fruits of his experience, the first being an account of his incarceration, and the second, published together with the first, an account of the return home. Put metaphorically, the first is the descent into hell, and the latter the ascent from it. They also become the primary statement of his life work, his confrontation with the event, and the ambition both to convey the experience precisely and accurately. But also, he wanted to ponder its implications for our understanding of the nature of man, of what he can

---

[1] Primo Levi, *Se questo è un uomo*. First published in 1947 in a small limited edition by a publishing which soon closed down. It was republished on a much larger scale in 1958 by Giulio Eanaudi, Torino. *If This is a Man*. Trans. Stuart Woolf. First published by The Orion Press in 1959, and under the title, *Survival in Auschwitz* in 1961. The page references given here are to the Penguin edition, 1993.

[2] It is referred to as the '[c]anonical text of Holocaust literature.' See David Patterson, Alan Berger and Sarita Cargas (eds.) *Encyclopaedia of Holocaust Literature* (Westport: Oryx Press, 2002).

do, not only for evil, but also in the move towards redemption. As a writer, a condition to which he had always aspired, he had found his subject. But as a writer too, he had no option but to deploy the instrument of language. And now he writes: 'Then for the first time we became aware that our language lacks words for this offence, the demolition of a man.' (32) That remains the challenge, to find the appropriate expressive means for this ultimate experience. In his own preface, he defines the purpose of his writing as '[a]n interior liberation. Hence its fragmentary character: the chapters have been written not in logical succession, but in order of urgency.' This is a new approach to documentary writing, jettisoning chronological sequence and alternative order in favour of a kind of musical scale, with the heaviest blasts opening the performance. And so he opens by posing the question of the nature of man, including a short poem, giving the book its title. Immediately, he raises the expressed doubt as regards the adequacy of the tool employed, which necessarily is the word itself. But, it can be seen that the doubt as expressed contains in itself the nub of the experience, and thus conveys its nature and ultimate pain. There is an internal need to tell this story to others, to communicate it and to ponder its meaning. Of central importance in this enterprise is the need for absolute veracity. And this work, together with Levi's many other works, has thus become a primary source for our understanding and knowledge of the camps.

The author starts by telling us of the division of Auschwitz into sections, and his particular incarceration in the Monowitz-Buna sector, which was supposed to be the production centre. Buna is a type of rubber, which the factory is purported to produce, so the whole outfit is known by this name. An important factor in the author's insistence on factually accurate reportage, is the lesson to be derived, that just as perfect happiness is unattainable, so is its antithesis. Not all doors can be closed together, and there always remains a residue of hope, even at the apparently lowest point of the spirit. This sector, Buna, allows for at least temporary survival. The Germans had discovered by this stage in the war that the rate of extermination had been so rapid that they had found themselves short of manpower for war production, and so decided to maximise this available slave labour potential, before the victims head for extinction. Levi, as a prisoner soon gets accustomed to the regime imposed on him, and to the fact of its arbitrariness. And he takes in the often-repeated motto: 'Hier ist kein warum' (Here there is no why). One must assume that everything is forbidden unless it is expressly permitted, which is the very reverse of the norm in the outside world. He learns (as do we) the topography of the *Lager*, and how the camp works. Everything, to its tiniest and most absurd detail, is regulated, so that life itself becomes a minefield of meaningless prohibitions, which must be adhered to for very survival. The rhythm of routine is predictable and painful, but unavoidable. They seem to be at the very bottom, but there is always a lower level that will then be reached. Regularly too, it is observed how the number of familiar faces declines, and how those that do go on, also decline into decrepitude.

Together with the precise description of everyday life in the camp, Levi attaches a reflection on the meaning of it all. Specifically, he is concerned with the question of how to retain any possible element of humanity within this murky hell. The whole object of the camp defies rationality. It is not to win the war, nor to promote production, and obviously not to care for the welfare of the prisoners. In the last case, the project is the reverse; everything here is designed to cause maximum pain, discomfort and confusion in the limited time available prior to final extinction. The orders are capricious, moving people about quite senselessly. The novice is in a state of terror and bewilderment. The procedures are unclear. There is a Babel of tongues. Orders of course are issued in German, a language that Levi only really picked up in the course of his incarceration (he had known some German before for purposes of his studies, but this did not include the spoken language). Life issues, such as logistical problems with clothing, food and the instruments required for basic living, are mysterious, hidden from the prisoners themselves. Of course, Levi's text is composed subsequent to the time of the actual experiences relayed, so it comes with analysis and reflection. His concern had been of course with physical survival, but an essential prior ingredient for its achievement, he surmises, is moral survival. Some actions may have seemed meaningless in overt practical terms, but were necessary for one's mental balance. This is all part of what he calls, being a 'man', that is, retaining one's humanity against all the odds. For example, to follow the written order to wash in order to keep clean could be regarded as absurd, as the order itself was clearly a slap in the face. The water was dirty, so immersion in it could produce no positive effect. Nevertheless, Levi insists, as he had learnt from his peers, and specifically from his older friend Steinlauf, that following such a human procedure was an absolute requirement for the sake of one's own dignity, and self-image. Thus one could still preserve that memory and essence: 'Precisely because the Lager was a great machine to reduce us to beasts, we must not become beasts.' (47) The other purpose of such survival was to be able afterwards '[t]o tell the story, to bear witness; and that to survive we must force ourselves to save at least the skeleton, the scaffolding, the form of civilization.'

Steinlauf is the first of many individuals mentioned in Levi's chronicles, whom the author not only observed, but from whom he learnt so much in terms of life skills. It was also necessary for Levi to realise that, even after such an experience, it is not solely the evil that emerges and is reclaimed, but the lessons that can be picked up from others of essential value. Much of Levi's writing is concerned with people, and a considerable proportion of his various books is devoted to portraits of those whom he encountered. Remarkably, but typically amongst the writers who have emerged from the 'concentrationary' experience, nothing else in their lives, neither before the entry into the camp, nor in what has followed, matches this in significance. In temporal terms, in Levi's case, the overall time spent imprisoned was not huge, around one and a half years, not so much as measured in relation to his total life span. But that is the difference between subjective and objective time. That particular one and a half years is time of another dimension, and it is that to which the author devotes his attention within what is the residue of his earthly days. The rest can be spent in meditation on the lessons picked up, what he has acquired and what he has failed to acquire. Levi would have been a writer whatever his experiences, and the fact that he is an Auschwitz survivor just determines his direction as a Holocaust writer. The material garnered though is not just death and evil, although the whole nature of Auschwitz naturally tends in that direction. The literary bent of the narrator also ensures a broader scope and intention for his pen. How others react, how they behave, and how he behaves, as well as what he might do, how, finally, all of this can be absorbed in his psyche, and written up. He becomes a chronicler, a witness, and one who draws conclusion after due reflection.

Levi's literary mentor is Dante. Levi writes in the Italian tradition, and so he has a model of the world as divided into good and evil, heaven and hell. Hell is the locus of his visitation, but he is also someone who has managed to emerge from there. But the composition of the evil place, the camp, is made up of details, all of which are vital for the prisoner. He has to hold on to his possessions, without which he will not be able to function, and thus, not to survive in this environment. He must not lose his shoes, his beret, his spoon, his bowl, and gloves. Survival in Auschwitz then is achieved by a specific technique that has to be learned through experience and suffering. Experience involves deprivation. He soon has to go to the 'Krankenbau', the infirmary, which is of course a parody of its declared function. Soon, he begins to hear about the selections and the crematoria, the gas; these things, amazingly, had been kept from such prisoners even by this late stage.

There is a distinction that comes about in Levi's analysis between body and spirit. This latter is not seen in traditionally religious terms, in relation to a deity, but rather in terms of man's non-physical capacity. Through what the brief respite that the infirmary has afforded him, he can reflect more deeply on the nature of man. One thing is certainly clear, more than ever under the Nazis; that life is extremely cheap, easily dispensable, and soon cast off. But that is common to all living things. What is more at stake here is the 'personality', the element that grants the essence of humanity to people: '[w]e have learnt that our personality is fragile, that it is much more in danger than our life.' (61) This realisation has only been made possible away from the curses and blows, in the twenty day withdrawal from the heat of the camp evil, offering an opportunity to rebuild the self anew. But the respite is of course brief, and the return to 'health' offers its own revenge. Everything has changed, as though he has just arrived; a new environment, new comrades, and back to the torture.

Levi is careful to itemise the subject matter, so that the reader knows precisely the headings treated. He deals with all aspects of camp life; 'treatment' of the sick, the nature of the 'work', the 'latrines', the 'market', the 'food'. To each item we append quotation marks, as each constitutes in fact a parody of the familiar nature of the item. The food, a sort of broth, which is in fact rather murky water, somewhat relieves the hunger, but induces swelling and brings about deformity. Human nature inherently seek purpose constantly and in everything. This is so here too, but, in the camp, that purpose is reduced, slimmed down. In fact, it has come down to the urge to stay alive till the Spring. The nature of the 'work' is fraudulent. The industrial complex, the Buna factory, officially earmarked for the production of rubber, in fact produced nothing: '[t]he Buna factory, on which the Germans were busy for four years and for which countless of us suffered and died, never produced a pound of synthetic rubber.' (79) And there are always enemies, if not the cold in the march towards the Spring, then the hunger, which is naturally constant, as it is man made, and the deprivation intended. The so-called 'market' is the focus of camp trade offs. As far as possible from the SS huts, exchanges take place of things that would normally neither be regarded as vital for existence or of no consequence. In reality, they could be both. For example, gold fillings are sometimes extracted from one's own teeth, ragged shirts, bread (taken from the ration), *mahorca* (crude tobacco), spoons (manufactured in the Buna, and used for trade). Anyone with any initiative can get hold of something, and then use it to trade in for something else, seemingly of greater value at that particular moment. But the ethical conclusion, which Levi ponders once more, is that all is permitted in this weird framework. Indeed, the accepted norms of society are set in reverse. Morality has become ambiguous, as it no longer bears the absolute quality expected of it.

Levi's most reflective chapter in the book carries the heading that was used later for another whole volume, 'The Drowned and the Saved'.[3] Here, the author poses the question of '[w]hether it is necessary or good to retain any memory of this exceptional

[3] Primo Levi, *I sommersi e i salvati* (Torino: Giulio Einaudi, 1986). *The Drowned and the Saved*, trans. Raymond Rosenthal (London: Michael Joseph, 1988; Abacus, 1988).

human state.' (93) The state referred to is the concentrationary condition, where many men are '[c]rushed against the bottom'. The question arises because we might, rationally be tempted to reply in the negative, if man is basically a pleasure-seeking creature. Why, after all, should we dwell on pain, and wallow in the memory of such awful experiences. However, as is clear from the author's own activity, Levi's reply is in the opposite vein, and he asserts [t]hat no human experience is without meaning or unworthy of analysis, and that fundamental values, even if they are not positive, can be deduced from this particular world which we are describing.' Moreover, the world that has been created here can be seen as a huge laboratory for '[a] gigantic biological and social experiment.' After all, we are observing man pressed to the ultimate limit, and can then infer conclusions about his nature, which otherwise would remain uncharted. Levi wishes to take into account the subtleties and gradations of types and shades, not to jump to extreme black and white conclusions (clearly, it would normally be thought that it is the black that is appropriate in this context). Nevertheless, he argues that there are two well differentiated types as indicated by the chapter title, which characterise the human species. The camp offers a perfect opportunity to observe this distinction, he argues, just because the restraints of normal society, the imposition of law, the protection of the weak, the limitation on the strong, are not in place. So people can go to the limit. They will even want to go to the limit, as the preponderance of the weak, becoming the drowned, the 'Mussulman',[4] will be to the advantage of the residue. In the camps, the prisoner is alone, and must make his (or

---

[4] It seems that Levi has slightly misunderstood the term, and so misspells it as 'Muselmann', puzzling that he can not understand why it is used to describe '[t]he weak, the inept, those doomed to selection.' (94, footnote) But the word simply means 'Muslim', on the basis of the observation that the nature of Islam was to 'submit' to the will of Allah.

her) own struggle for life in an isolated condition. Here, it is the strong who survive, those who assert their will, and precisely do not submit. It is they who are willing to jettison the previously held societal norms in order to gain immediate personal benefit. They will also evince greater discipline and even an iron will. Such people will attempt to curry favour with the relevant authorities, and so entrench themselves in a more secure position. Levi makes an effort to outline the nature of a potential survivor, one who is 'saved', although we may be sceptical of the rules applied, and descry a lack of consistency. Sometimes, such individuals are marked for their empathy, but on other occasions, they seem to be conspicuously self-seeking. It may be that the whole subject needs to be examined afresh.

Our biographical concern takes us to the question of to which category Levi himself belonged. Was he one of the saved or one of the drowned? The fact of his survival informs us that he must be classed as one of the former. But the author himself casts doubt on this. He holds that he is decidedly a 'drowned'. He is too delicate, too introspective, and not sufficiently single minded: 'I know that I am not made of the stuff of those who resist, I am too civilized, I still think too much, I use myself up at work.' (109) But there is a way out. That is to become a specialist, which is to be needed by the SS, and he can become a 'specialist' by passing a Chemistry exam. Thus he joins the newly formed 'Chemical Kommando'.

In the meantime, another factor asserts itself more and more. As time moves on, and we pass through the Summer of 1944, the camp work is on the point of disintegration. Allied bombing penetrates further, and parts of the camp are constantly having to be reconstructed. Any effort made in the production of rubber in the Buna is now abandoned. One thing however does not abate, and that is the killing process. This is ever more accelerated, especially now with the arrival and annihilation of Hungarian Jewry, following the German occupation of Hungary. And there is still a Winter to come, in which the struggle for life is further intensified. What keeps Levi going is the sense that there is still a model of probity, an existent life to preserve the image of a man within. In retrospect, we know that each day of struggle was important as the defeat of the Nazi empire was imminent and inevitable. As the camp becomes more overcrowded, the word of 'selection' spreads. The selection will reduce the population of the Lager, and each one feels that his end has now been announced. The chimneys of Birkenau are working overtime. All the inmates have been reduced to skin and bones, and are on the verge of becoming 'Mussulmänner'. But Levi passes the great selection of October 1944, more by chance than by design. The object of the selections is primarily to reduce the numbers in the camp in order to make room for more, rather than to preserve the fittest.

Twenty-one of the Italians have survived beyond October from the initial ninety-six. They are pressed between the German need for accelerated murder and the approach of the Russians. The inmates feel filthy and demeaned, on the verge of extinction, less than human beings, particularly contemptible in the company of the women of the Buna. And some of the worst of the experiences are not described, barely even mentioned. But now, with the Russians nearing, the camp has to be evacuated. The imminent collapse of the German world is perceptible. For the evacuation, Levi again finds himself in the infirmary, sick with scarlet fever, and by the time that he gets out, the camp has been abandoned. He flees then as a patient. He is offered a slice of bread, and it is then that he realises the implication; the Lager is dead (166). A gesture such as this, '[t]he first human gesture', would have been inconceivable within the spirit of Auschwitz itself. Dawn breaking on 20 January presages the liberation. The rest of the book takes

154

the form of a diary, ending with 27 January, the day that the Russian troops arrive.

The Way Back

Levi's primary work, *If This is a Man*, might never have been written, had it not been for the counterpoint potential of the successor statement, *The Truce*. As we have indicated (above), the former is the path into hell, and the latter marks the way out. Obviously, there is not much sense of untroubled joy for the survivors, wrecked and reduced, with the embers of a world disintegrated all around. But, as a contrast, this can be seen as something resembling Dante's *Il paradiso*.

The Germans tried to evacuate the healthy prisoners to Buchenwald and Mauthausen, although the rapid Soviet advance forced them to leave this task incomplete. Together with Levi in the infirmary were 800 patients, of which 500 had died by the time of the Russian incursion. A further 200 died in the days following. For the camp inmates, the invading Soviet forces were seen as 'messengers of peace' (188). Paradoxically, it was the prisoners themselves who felt shame, again the shame of the 'offence', the shame of the crimes committed by other human beings: '[t]he shame the Germans did not know, that the just man experiences at another man's crime; the feeling of guilt that such a crime should exist...' Only 'we' (i.e. those who have undergone the experience) have '[b]een able to grasp the incurable nature of the offence, that spreads like a contagion.' Also paradoxically, after the dreadful suffering and casual and constant killing, he now, on liberation, felt closer to death than during the whole period of capture. Eventually, paralysed, he is dragged off in a cart, and it is only now that he discovers that, since he had been at Buna-Monowitz, he had really been unaware of the enormous dimensions of 'Auschwitz proper'. Now they were being cared for by Russian nurses, but also cleansed and in a sense deprived of their recently acquired identity. What Levi is trying to convey here is the sense of a reverse of fortune, with the new life force streaming in and replacing the all-pervasive death of incarceration. This could signal the recovery of the sense of his total opus, which is, what it means to be a man: 'the dying were dead, in all the others life was beginning to flow again tumultuously.' (197)

The journey home is indirect, tortuous, and interrupted, and on it, he learns not only about the conditions pertaining at the tail end of the war and the German retreat, but also about human nature. As before, the author retains an enormous curiosity about the variety of human kind, and its variability under changing conditions. The voyage itself lacks logical direction. In order to go South West (in the direction of Italy, they (he is accompanied) start moving North and East, via Cracow and Katowice, to a transit camp. The bustle all around is chaotic and ravaged, still in the throes of a prolonged and savage conflict, and following a ruthless occupation, now controlled by another foreign power. But still, it offers an absolute contrast to the Lager, as it is certainly life. Levi notes the vitality of characters, the freedom of movement with all its problematics, and the now renewed prospects. People around were scavengers, cheats and thieves, determined to get the better of you, and prey off the weaker in a very much reduced economy. But, at least they were not on the whole engaged in systematic slaughter, so that we know that all the rules had been reversed, and that we are now back in a state of relative normality.

The narrator/author tries to convey the feeling of the war coming to an end. Europe is exhausted, apparently emptied of its resources, and May 8 marks the end, (although of course there is still the enormous matter of Japan). The journey has to continue, and Levi hopes to make his way now via Odessa. But inexplicably (nothing is ever adequately explained), at Zhmerinka, they are held up, and later, they have to proceed in the opposite direction, away from Odessa, Northwards. In the meantime, throughout all the journey and later too, all sorts of people are encountered, and minutely observed. These observations make up a good deal of the content for Levi's later books. A long stay at Starye Dorogi, where food is relatively plentiful, gives him a chance to build up his strength. The train then moves onwards, this time in the correct Southerly direction, forward to the Romanian border at Iasi, then through Brasov on the Hungarian frontier, and on to Austria. Even then, they do not move forward directly to Italy, but divert through Munich. Here, Levi receives the shock of being, for the first time, amongst the 'Herrenvolk' in Germany proper, in their own country, and he speculates, as he did constantly throughout his life, on how much was known by the general population of what had been done in their name. He arrives back in Turin on October 17, to be haunted by the imagined dawn cry of 'Wstawàch', meaning: 'Get up'. This is a cry which has accompanied the author metaphorically ever since, as he feels that it is his life function to become aware of his own memory, and of what has happened to him. It is also seen as his function to tell the story, as he has done here, in cold factuality and sober tone.

The Reprise

Levi's subsequent works are all autobiographical one way or another, leading up to the incarceration and later reflections on its meaning and implications. *The Periodic Table*[5] is actually an autobiography, although it takes the form of a narrative expansion of Mendeleyev's periodic table, where each chemical element itemised suggests some episode from the past. This is an autobiography with pen portraits of those people with whom he had come into contact, and who had done much to shape his life and thought. He builds up his Piedmontese Jewish background, and his own identity on the fringes of Jewish and Italian consciousness. And he attempts to give an account of his life, the external forces that shaped him, the momentous events taking place, but also his own tendencies and predilections. For example; why did he choose Chemistry as his field of study, his career, and his obsession too. He says: '[f]or me, chemistry represented an indefinite cloud of future potentialities which enveloped my life to come in black volutes torn by fiery flashes, like those which had hidden Mount Sinai...another key to the highest truths.' (22-3) The discipline of this science constituted an antidote to Fascism, 'clear and distinct and verifiable at every step, and not a tissue of lies and emptiness, like the radio and newspapers.' (42) He also explains the sort of person he is, and the character that granted a particular shape to the nature of his writing. He is a storyteller, says the author: 'I am one of those people to whom many things are told.' (68) He thus sees himself as a kind of tape recorder, setting down other people's stories, whilst, at the same time, filling us in on his position within the overall frame. So many of the twenty-one episodes of the book, i.e.

---

[5] *The Periodic Table* (London: Michael Joseph, 1985). *Il sistema periodico* Torino: Giulio Einaudi, 1975).

the separate elements, are stories told by others. This is a different way of telling a single story, a tapestry composed of various strands, which nevertheless is conflated into a united whole. We must be invited to conclude that just as the world is both one and many, comprising the elements, so humanity is divergent, diverse, and yet, necessarily integrated. There are many languages, stories, contexts, histories and temperaments. But they have to interact, and that interaction is the content of a larger, more inclusive story.

Levi characterises this book as being neither a chemical treatise, nor really an autobiography, but rather a micro history of a trade. (224) Every chemist, he argues, must have tied his destiny to one of the elements. This is more than ever so in the case of carbon, which speaks to all. This element is the catalyst for life, as '[i]t is the only element that can bind itself in long stable chains without a great expense of energy, and for life on earth precisely long chains are required.' (226-7) Thus it is the key to life. The gas, carbon dioxide, is the raw material of growth. Levi's astonishment then is at the way that life has come about, in this arbitrary fashion, and that this has resulted in the very specific human being that is the author himself, who has produced these particular signs, which compose the text before us. Into this is inserted another part of the author's story, the story that is told in *If This is a Man*, and around which the personal story, crisis and tragedy of his biography was played out. But we are also told an essential part of the story with which we are not familiar, of, for example, how he joined a partisan group to fight Fascist rule, how he was betrayed and captured on December 13, 1943 by the Fascists of Saló, who were under the protection of Nazi Germany (131). We also read again of how he learnt to acquire the reversed ethical system by leaning how to survive in Auschwitz, that is by stealing, and in general by learning to protect his interests by any means available. (131)

We can best understand Levi's work as a dialectic played out against the background of his life. His biography is the thesis, a lad buffeted by a cruel fate, and emerging from it. The antithesis is his chemistry, the analysis of the discipline that is based on observation and reasoning power. It is not clear which one emerges as dominant; perhaps both do at different points of time, and the struggle goes on. The most considered summation of the lessons to be learned from these awful experiences is the book by Levi, which adopts the title of one of the chapters in *If This is a Man*, which is *The Drowned and the Saved*, written shortly before his death.[6] As is often the way in this sort of case, the question posed by the survivor himself addresses the nature of survival, and of what it consists. How did this survival come about, and what ends can it serve? Levi has divided the victims into the two categories, of those capable of survival strategy and the others (the vast majority) who are not. But the word 'saved' in the salvationist sense has a supernatural connotation. If you are saved, you are necessarily, in the literal meaning of the term, saved by someone and for something. It is a verb used here in the passive mode, and there must be a subject outside to support it. Also, this division into categories must be shared by humanity at large. On the other hand, it must be said that to be 'saved', in Levi's terms, has no implication of grace. Quite the contrary, for the author, it is the 'drowned' who are the true witnesses, those who were annihilated. It is amongst these that were to be found the few who resisted, those who attempted to heed ethical imperatives, who tried to help others, or to save some dignity in themselves and for themselves.

What can be done by such survivors as Levi? Precisely, to relay the event. It had been a recurrent nightmare of the persecuted that they were going to disappear without trace, and that

---

[6] See note 3.

even if they were to be in a position later to tell their story, they would not be believed. Neither their story, nor the story as told by others, would be attended to, because, firstly, it was a story too dreadful for human ears, and secondly, that it transcended credulity. So, the least that Levi can see fit to attempt now is to tell and to retell, to fill in the gaps, to challenge the sceptical, to answer the questions of how and why. He is a writer, so he must write books, and this must be his subject. This subject is not only what had been carried out by the perpetrators, but also what had been effected by those complicit. Certainly this applied to the German nation, at the very least, as they must have had more than an inkling of what was taking place. And yet they chose, for whatever motives, to keep silent: 'Without this cowardice the greatest excesses would not have been carried out, and Europe and the world would be different today.' (4) These were the passive collaborators. But there were also those who were active; not only the individuals who operated the camps, the SS and the guards, the *Wehrmacht* too, but those who supplied the camps, who manufactured the striped uniforms for the prisoners, the industrialists who assembled the crematoria, as well as those who supplied the poisonous gas. These might have been active Nazis, who believed in the policy being pursued, or maybe, at the best, simple folk anxious to save themselves.

Who are the reliable witnesses? Not necessarily the victims themselves, as their particular corner did not really offer the best perspective to view the larger picture. Could someone so deprived and tortured be expected to know what was going on some miles away, or even in other parts of the same camp? On the other hand, those who were 'privileged' were compromised, as, in return for their privileges, they must have sacrificed an element of objectivity and truth. *The Drowned and the Saved* constitutes an attempt to present the sort of testimony needed, a corrective to some of the myths that had attached themselves to the events: 'This book means to contribute to the clarification of some aspects of the Lager phenomenon which still appear obscure.' (9) In tone, it even seems to be a corrective to the earlier volumes and memoirs. Paradoxically, for one who is now further removed from the nightmarish events themselves, as was the case for the author, the mood is darker. But perhaps this is not so surprising. *If This is a Man*, so close to the war and the Holocaust in time, must have borne the marks of relief at the act of liberation. Everything must have been such a welcome contrast, an absolute distinction that should never be forgotten between slavery and freedom. But now, that past is being deliberately resurrected and inspected for sober consideration, and we have to absorb its lessons, bleak as they may be. For Levi, despite all the horrors of the post-war phase, the Nazi concentration camp system remains a '[u]nicum, both in extent and quality.' (10)

Levi is careful to distinguish between types of testimony and their reliability, both on the part victims and of their oppressors, and he was prepared to assign authority to both only in varying degrees. But still he very carefully holds the two separate in terms of moral responsibility. He always distances himself from the type of fashionable generalisation that: 'we are all victims', or, conversely, that: 'we are all oppressors'. Degrees of responsibility and culpability must be carefully made and borne in mind. There is talk here neither of forgetting nor of forgiveness. On the contrary, it is of prime importance to remember and to transmit the memory. The crime was appalling and unique, and must be analysed, recalled, and then communicated to those who could have no knowledge of it, or to those whose knowledge in this respect is imperfect and defective. A deed once done lives on, and its effects are compounded with time, not erased. Similarly, the roles once played cannot be reversed by some sleight of hand: 'We do not wish to abet confusions, small-change Freudianism, morbidities and indulgences. The oppressor remains what he is, and so does the victim. They are not interchangeable...' (13) Levi is very concerned at the degree of mystification and obfuscation employed by the criminals in their efforts to disclaim culpability. The usual refrain echoed by the accused is of course that they were just obeying orders, and that they had no option but to carry these out, if they wished to stay alive. Others deny the events themselves. The author analyses the process of distortion and the degree of bad faith evinced by those charged, and on the part of those indeed responsible. In effect, what is demanded here overall is a recognition of responsibility, the admission that human beings own their actions, and that they are normally in charge of themselves. It can be observed particularly in the case of such initiators and star criminals as Höss and Eichmann, that they acted freely, willingly, even enthusiastically, and of their own initiative. But Levi does still naturally recognise the capacity of the human mind for self-deception, and how such people can believe what they themselves project at another level. This sort of thing can be done and frequently is, with another intent. For example, people can believe in something that they want to believe in. This is the nature of wish fulfilment. So the picture of the human being, involving the jagged image of the psyche, is complex. But that must not distract us from the main issue, which is the recognition of the facts as they are and were, as well as of the fact that these things were carried out by a conscious and conscientious person.

Levi's general caveat is also turned against himself. He after all is writing long after the event, and, like everyone else, he must possess an imperfect memory, suffering from natural all too human failings. As with everyone else's account then, his must also be subject to verification and checking. But now (that is, at the time of writing), there is a substantial literature on the subject of his concern, and he finds that what he has recorded remains in general consonance with the drift of other accounts. He finds that his texts bear all the hallmarks of determined honesty and a drive towards the understanding of human nature in all its complexity. Such an aspiration would be rendered meaningless if it were not impelled by a recognition of the maximal degree of truth, truth both to the object of his enquiry and to himself.

Levi is concerned with the system of the Lager, as the Lager serves as a kind of laboratory, sinister as it may be, for his investigations. The reason for this is of course random, that is, it happened by chance that this was the greatest circumstance of his life. It was an exquisitely painful experience, but it did provide the writer with the opportunity to observe the nature of the creature, i.e. the human being, in its most extreme condition. The objective of the Lager was to reduce the 'opponents' to their ultimate state, and this objective was indeed achieved. It is a myth, argues Levi, that Nazism sanctifies its victims: '[o]n the contrary, it degrades them, it makes them similar to itself. (25) He is entirely unsentimental about what happened to the victims, and specifically to those who managed somehow to withstand the wholesale killing machine. And this generalisation, he fully realises, must also apply to himself, both as a victim and as a survivor.

To sum up the principal thrust and to get to the heart of the Nazi enterprise is Levi's objective. The purpose of that enterprise: '[w]as to destroy Jews, and, beginning in 1943, the population in Auschwitz was composed of ninety to ninety-five percent Jews.' (35) Our knowledge of that must be made more precise, and a judgment made possible. Who are the guilty? This question indeed must receive a highly qualified analysis and reply. But it cannot be sidestepped. There are many guilty people, but some are more guilty than others. There are also various shades of grey; those who bear much blame, but whose capacity to exercise free choice was restricted. This is discussed in the chapter, 'The Grey Zone'. Much of Levi's book is concerned with a confrontation with nuances. But this should never be confused with the facile reduction of all to the same level of responsibility.

In another sense, the 'drowned' are all those who have been through the experience of the Lager, on whichever side. The perpetrators are morally drowned, guilty of the most horrific crimes, and rightly condemned in the most outright terms, and by any form of justice available. But the victims are also the drowned. Those who did not survive were 'drowned' physically, exterminated. Those who survived have been drowned in another sense, and doubly. Firstly, by their terrible experience, and secondly, by the shame of survival, bearing witness to the 'offence' of the perpetrators. Ethically, they must be contrasted absolutely, as night from day. But they both remain permanently scarred. No one touched by this event can escape, so that the term 'saved' can only be used in a very provisional sense.

VIII

AND SO IT GOES ON: LATER LITERATURE
OF THE HOLOCAUST

A New Naturalism

There can be no more effective way of responding to the Holocaust in literature than by presenting the facts as simply and as truly as possible. Some survivors of the experience have aspired to carry this out, and continue to do so. One such is the Jewish Czech writer, Arnošt Lustig (b. 1926), a prolific author of both short and long fiction, as well as a filmmaker. He went through both Theresienstadt and Auschwitz, spent some periods in Israel, and following the suppression of the brief Prague Spring in 1968, settled in the USA, where he now lives in Washington DC. Typical of his direct and naturalistic manner is the collection of short fiction, *Diamonds of the Night*.[1] The stories report without adornment, conveying an authentic impression of the texture of life under Nazi occupation, highlighting, in the main, the plight of children and the elderly, i.e. the most vulnerable and helpless members of society.

---

[1] Arnošt Lustig, *Diamonds of the Night*, trans Jeanne Némcová (London: Quartet Books, 1989); orig. pub. as *Démanty noci* (Prague, 1958).

The first story, for example, 'The Lemon', is set in occupied Lodz (although the author is Czech, the scene of action in his work is often Poland) at the time of the 'actions', the roundups, and the transports. Through the specifics of the plot here we learn of how life was lived, and concretely, how much investment of effort in this case was placed upon a single lemon, in the hope that it might relieve the suffering of the main character, Ervin's sister, who is so lacking in vitamins. We note the pathetic sources of survival, the low value placed on human life, the prevalent starvation, the proliferation of disease, the nature of casual death, and the way that life was constantly risked for the sake of the most minimal food. Ervin is literally the 'breadwinner' of the family, charged with doing his absurd best to bring some sort of succour to his mother and sister. He, in his turn, is willing to undergo the most demeaning experiences, here scraping the gold from his dead father's mouth, in order to have the bartering power to get some food for the family. At the end, all he can do is weep, and that silently.

Lustig's stories are told graphically, and, in a sense, cinematically. The writing is economical, abundant in dialogue and movement. Narratorial comment is minimal, as is the exposition. The reader has to pick up the sense and the context quickly from the material as derived from the dialogue and the described action. Since the raw material is so horrific, there is no need to lay on any supplementary emotive content. The plot speaks for itself. The emotion will naturally be transmitted to the reader. In the above, we know that the lemon is being invested with life saving properaties well beyond its inherent capacities. Similarly, the 'hero' of the story is being asked by his mother, and, by implication, his sister too, to achieve things way beyond his powers. The story should be one of merely staying alive, but we know, on the basis of familiar reality, that this will turn out to be a story of attempted, and, no

doubt, failed survival. Many of the stories do not turn on the heroism of fighting or attempted escape, but on the pathetic struggle,
with altogether inadequate means, for life, at least for a few more
hours. We hover between life and death, and the latter is imminent. But we do not have to have this spelt out in explicit detail, as
this is indicated by the nature of the reportage.

The stories plunge us directly into the thick of the action
without preliminaries, and we pick up the necessary information to
make sense of what is happening through that action. The author
takes the reader into his confidence, but *ab initio* assumes a considerable degree of familiarity with the background without the need
for explication. In the story, 'The Second Round', we see that life
itself is a lottery. The story is about drawing lots, and that action
becomes a metaphor for the nature of the existence under these
conditions. The one who draws the shortest twig has to do the job,
which is to get some food from the supply car, an extremely risky
enterprise, since, if he were to be seen, he would be shot like a dog
by the Germans, immediately. They had not eaten for six days.
The lot falls to the one who is known, provocatively, as 'Marquis',
and the description of his race for the loaf seems to take as long as
the incident in real time. And the conversation that goes on within
his own head is longer still. They are all awaiting death, like the
relatives of Marquis, who '[w]ent up the chimney'. (54) He is
caught by the *Scharführer*, but has managed to throw the loaf to his
friends, unnoticed by him. In this particular case, the friends inter-
vene, and, in the resulting confusion, specifically in the German
officer's mind, the incident is closed. The little fellow had in fact
saved Marquis's life for the moment, because he did not think it
fair that the one who had carried out the project as a result of a
lottery, should get nothing of the bread. Of such stuff is the typical
Lustig story made, and this is the life under Nazi occupation on
the road to almost certain extinction. Marquis's thoughts (as repre-

sented by italicised print) are interwoven with the ongoing action. The narrative focus, like a ciné camera, moves from one figure to the next, taking us forward in time, along what is in fact an extremely short span. The thread of life is very fine, and the border between that and death almost imperceptible. But the moment of death is almost lived through. In the interim however, facets of character, hitherto unsuspected, suddenly peep out into the sunlight to extend another shade to an otherwise totally bleak surface.

The story, 'The White Rabbit', takes the subject as a metaphor for the human psyche. The lesson that they should learn from their own experience as well as that of others, is that they should trust nobody (68). It is set in the Theresienstadt concentration camp, a pseudo Jewish town. The central figure in the story wants to show the girl with encephalitis, whom he knows as Flea (he does not know her real name), his lovely white rabbit. But when he tries to retrace her, he is informed that she is 'elsewhere'. No comment is necessary. In 'The Old Ones and Death', also set in Theresienstadt, talk takes place between the old people. But some had recently had parents. Now, these are dead, gassed, as are the children. For the Nazis, the old and the young, as well as the sick, the maimed, and even those with spectacles, are for immediate extermination. This is life under the Nazis, in the ghettos, in the concentration camps, and, of course, in the death camps. Such a picture requires no rhetorical expansion.

Transposition of Expectations

The writer has felt that he has to confront the past as represented by the Holocaust and its enormous implications for our understanding of humanity, not only meaningfully but uniquely. If the literature produced is to justify itself, it must make a contribution in terms of new understanding or new approaches, otherwise why do it. Much of the material produced then revolves around the issue of novelty, ever attempting to see the event afresh, and to reverse expectations as we approach the subject as though it had not been previously encountered. Such a novel is *Sophie's Choice*[2] by the American author, William Styron (b. 1925). In this novel, the author takes us through a long and complex story, related by a narrator, whose biography is very close to the author's own. Born in 1925, Stingo, as he is commonly know, from Virginia, comes to New York, in search of a career as a writer, and after a debilitating debut working for a publisher, moves to a rooming house in Flatbush. The novel opens in 1947, but covers an extensive range of the narrator's life, and is written in distant retrospect. Thus the narrator, a Protestant Southerner, finds himself in what he describes as Jewish territory: '[a]nother lean and lonesome young Southerner wandering amid the Kingdom of the Jews.' (9)

The Holocaust content of the novel derives from the story of the other tenants whose company Stingo shares, specifically that of the Polish beauty, Sophie Zawistowska, who is the lover of Nathan Landau. Sophie, a Catholic, is a survivor of Auschwitz, and our expectations are reversed in this confrontation with a Christian victim of Auschwitz, now in a masochistic relationship with the highly disturbed Jewish 'torturer'. The most significant section of the book is the framed account of Auschwitz, and the horrific nature of the 'choice' that Sophie has to make, when she is forced to select only one of her two children for life, otherwise condemning both to death. The account of the camp itself leans heavily on the apologetic testimony of Rudolf Höss himself, *Commandant of*

---

[2] William Styron, *Sophie's Choice* (London: Corgi Books, 1981); orig. pub. by Jonathan Cape (London, 1979).

Auschwitz, and therefore, in a sense, it incorporates the view of the one of the chief perpetrators of the genocide. So we have the perspective of the Commandant, a Polish Christian victim in a death camp targeted principally at Jews, and the whole overseen by the 'objective' outsider, the Virginian Stingo. The lovely Sophie (her beauty is constantly stressed by everyone around, and specifically by the narrator), was not only a victim at Auschwitz, but she seems to renew her status as victim in the Jewish environment of post war New York.

Much of the framed material of the book, and its very heart, derives from Sophie's own account of her past, in Cracow, her native city, and then later, in Warsaw, before Auschwitz. Much of that account, as relayed to the narrator, constitutes an attempt to question the stereotype of Polish anti-Semitism as the sole current in Polish life. She has a nostalgia for what she sees as the golden period between the wars. And she, after all, is a more reliable witness than the provincial Nathan, who can only rely on second-hand reports and inherited prejudices. But has this reliable witness been tainted by association with the perpetrators, and to what extent is her witness honest and credible? And is the reliance on Nathan as innocent as we might first assume? Certainly, she regards him as '[s]avior...and destroyer as well.' (184) Her status in Auschwitz was not of course like that of the Jews. She had been trapped for a relatively minor offence, smuggling meat into Warsaw; nothing near as terrible as being Jewish. But there always seems to be more to it, as she implies to Stingo, whom she makes into a sort of confessor substitute in her abandoned Catholic faith. She has been closely associated with Höss no less, and her representation of him, as filtered in the novel's narrative, touched on the human. He is presented not as a sadist, but as a crazed bureaucrat, devoted to duty and the obligation to carry out the unquestioned Nazi plan. Sophie is saved through her knowledge of the

German language and her competence as a secretary, and so can work for the Commandant, translating his correspondence, editing and typing. As we shall see, she is viewed (by herself and perhaps by others) as tainted by her ambiguous status and activities. And there lies the nub of the novel. The larger lie which Sophie had attempted to live, until she confessed it to Stingo, was that her father had been a Liberal. In fact he was a rampant racist and Jew hater, author of a pamphlet in German, bearing the title: 'Die polnische Judenfrage: Hat der Nationalsozialismus die Antwort?' (The Polish Jewish Question: Has National Socialism the Answer?)

It is not the case that Styron equates the treatment of the Jews by the Nazis in the death camps with that of other victims, and that Sophie is presented to exemplify this. On the contrary, the narrator points out that from early April 1943, Birkenau was almost exclusively reserved for the murder of Jews. Festering in the brains of the Nazi high command was the obsessive need to exterminate the totality of the Jewish population under their control, and Birkenau was to become the instrument in the implementation of this project. Styron recognises the 'dual function' of Auschwitz as a totality; mass murder and slave labour. Only, this latter had the peculiar characteristic of being constantly expendable, as the slaves were not built to last, and the labour function thus became ancillary. Styron is right about this, invoking Richard Rubenstein, although in other attempts at reversal of expectations he is decidedly wrong. As, for example, in his absurdly wayward, eccentric and unsupported assertion that Hans Frank, Nazi Governor General of Poland, was Jewish. (334).[3] The danger with the

---

[3] Op. cit. In regard to Sophie's father it is said that he '[s]ought to offer his services to the Governor General, Hitler's friend Hans Frank (a Jew, *mirabile dictu* – though few at the time knew it...' It is notoriously difficult to prove a negative, but there is absolutely no evidence for this assertion, and runs completely counter to what is known of Frank's career. He defended Hitler, as a lawyer, on

acceptance of such a loose borderline between factuality and fiction is that one may invade the territory of the other, and here such a statement is made with the full authority of the authorial voice, as though it be accepted fact. There is also the charge that such an aside is presumably not dropped just casually, as though incidental but not of particular significance. This comment must be purposeful, in its context and the effect, if not the intention, is malign. The distinction between Jewish and gentile victims is by no means overlooked. The Polish martyr, Wanda, says: ' "All are victims in Poland – but Jews are victims of victims." ' (629) Overall, the book is written with burning intensity, and presents a vital narrative, in which Sophie is the principal figure, interwoven with the narrator's own situation as a very young tyro, beginning to learn the ways of the world.

One of the features that makes the work so readable is the manner in which, very gradually yet quite realistically, more and more information becomes available to the reader about the truth of what happened in Sophie's life. It is at a fairly late stage that we (through what is told to Stingo) are informed that Sophie had a son, Jan, with her at Auschwitz. In fact, Sophie had had two children, Jan and Eva, and the terrible secret is what gives the novel its title. Her entry into Auschwitz had been marked by selection at the beginning of April 1943, the period when it was decided that Birkenau would be reserved for the total extermination of the Jews. Thus, only non-Jews would have the 'privilege' of going through a selection process. A diabolical scheme is hatched by the doctor in

---

numerous occasions, before 1933 too, and made the notorious statement in a speech on 16 December 1941: 'I ask nothing of the Jews except that they should disappear.' Post bellum, he sought reconciliation with the Catholic Church, dissociated himself from the Nazi ideology, but was executed following the Nuremberg trials. See Robert Wistrich, *Who's Who in Nazi Germany*, first pub. by Weidenfeld and Nicolson (London, 1982).

charge of the 'Selection', who, on hearing that Sophie is a Catholic, offers her the choice of saving one of her children, decreeing that otherwise, both would have to go. (642) Thus, the Nazi revenge on the part of a lapsed Catholic, the doctor, is to implant an awful sin into a victim, and thus create a shared guilt. This was now not only Sophie's guilt, but her lasting shame too, that, in addition to everything else, she had in a sense chosen to send Eva into the gas. More than anything else, she had yearned to be free of the past. But, as we see from the dénouement, this proves impossible. After an alliance and an affair with Stingo, and voyage to the South, she is drawn back to her nemesis, to the sick Nathan. In a wild Walpurgisnacht, they commit suicide together, and Stingo is left to embark on his independent path.

A Polyvocal Narrative

Experiments in the novel abound in order to intensify the impact, as well as to investigate a mystery from various angles. Nowhere is this more manifest than in narrative approaches to the Holocaust, an episode in history which seems to demand greater elasticity than is usual. *The White Hotel*[4] by D. M. Thomas is a case in point, presenting a story by separate voices in different media, a case history, a poem, a reconstruction of the Babi Yar massacre, already rendered by Anatoli Kuznetsov, itself based on existing documentation. The novel is a patchwork quilt, made up of a correspondence to which Sigmund Freud is party, a sort of confessional erotic prose poem, relating the affair between Freud's patient, Lisa Erdman, and Freud's son. Her journal covers the same ground prosaically, relating their affair on the train and in the

---

[4] D. M. Thomas, *The White Hotel* (London: Penguin Books, 1981).

'white hotel', (so pure, so hospitable, a sort of paradise. 'Nothing is sinful here', asserts an old nun, 'because of the Spring.' 72), then psychoanalytic case histories, followed by the sickening horror of the Babi Yar slaughter. The novel ends with a dream sequence. The narrative imitates the life of the unconscious, mingling dream and wakefulness, past and present, reality and fantasy, natural and supernatural, fact and fiction. The narrative structure breaks down barriers of time, place and literal possibility, as well as generic divisions.

The novel interweaves psychoanalysis in a historical perspective with the specific case of Lisa Erdman. Her fantasies of lust come together with the constant preoccupation with violent death, and the 'white hotel' is the scene of both. Passionate love is made there, and the hotel is burned to the ground. As seen by Freud, Lisa's case, mysterious pains on her left side, represents hysteria and sexual repression. But it is also laced with yearnings for death. The section, 'Frau Anna G.' is, as it were, presented by Freud at around the time of his formulation of the death instinct. His book, *Beyond the Pleasure Principle*, dates from 1920, and tries to account for the observed phenomenon that people seem not to be content with pleasure alone, as was first thought, and rather develop a mechanism of repetition compulsion, driving them back to their origins, i.e. towards death. But the psychoanalyst is satisfied, in the Erdman case, that he has worked a cure with his patient.

We see Lisa later, in 1929, towards the end of her operatic career, at the age of 39, singing the role of Tatiana in *Eugene Onegin* as an understudy for the renowned Vera Serebryakova in La Scala, Milan, opposite Victor, Vera's husband. She speculates on where her actual homeland is. Is it the Ukraine where she is born, or perhaps Poland, the birthplace of her mother. She herself has lived the last twenty years in Vienna. But she seems to move back towards the Ukraine, conducting a dance of love and death, of ultimate eroticism and facing maximal cruelty in a renewed confrontation with her Catholicism. She feels that she had lived a life of repression, and the 'half Jewish' part is liable to bubble up, although that had also been suppressed following an incident of violent anti-Semitism. From that time on, she views being Jewish as a terrible crime (169, in her letter to Freud), and she hides that part of herself. She is death obsessed, and has to sing the *Liebestod*.

The climax comes following her decision to return to Kiev at the invitation of Victor to join him, some time after Vera's death. Strange to think of a voluntary repatriation to the nightmare of the Soviet Union, and of course Victor is imprisoned. Lisa is now living with Victor's son Kolya (her stepson). The next chapter takes place under Nazi occupation, specifically to the roundup of Jews on 29 September 1941, a week after the takeover of Kiev. Kolya had to go; he is 'Jewish', son of a Jewish father, and Lisa goes with him. A horrific scenario is being enacted at the notorious site known as Babi Yar, a huge ravine and now host to an enormous massacre. They are all being shot, 30,000 in one day, a quarter of a million altogether. The narrator reflects that so many years later, there is no memorial. The surrealistic epilogue, entitled 'The Camp', proceeds from the dying mind of Lisa. She and Kolya together are now in a 'beautiful world' (226), and arrive at an oasis. They seem to be in a wondrous Israel, the Israel of visions and dreams rather than the reality of a Middle Eastern land. Now scenes from her life came crowding in her, forming a collective reconciliation with the past and with her mother and father. Only now does she realise that her pains had disappeared, and she seems to be genuinely cured. Thus, death and peace have come together, and created a permanent unity. The masses that had gathered for the slaughter at Babi Yar had become the camp of immigrants to a welcoming Israel.

Thomas's novel is both experimental and controversial. It strives to combine elements from different sources, existing historical material, fragments of biography, correspondence, case studies, fact and fiction. Each chapter deals with a different episode of Lisa's life, culminating in her horrific death, and a climax is achieved with a dream. Dreams form much of the content of this work, whose focus is both the history of psychoanalysis, and the conjoining of *eros* and *thanatos*. It is clear why the author should seek the fulcrum of his theme in the Holocaust, that ultimately surreal nightmare. But that was a nightmare from which the sleeper did not wake up.

Overcoming the Past

The second generation in Germany had to come to terms with its recent past just as the Jews had to. But this of course is a very different story. The generation of their parents had not merely fought a war; that would be a common feature for the majority of mankind. They had conducted a campaign of unprecedented, horrific and unprovoked cruelty. These moreover were the very people who were still in power, the cadre of politicians, lawyers, soldiers, and, above all, parents, who were still responsible for governance. Where were the Nazis, if they were not among us, those who had formed the overwhelming body of the population until so recently? How could they so suddenly have disappeared? And another question also had to be raised. Who are we? We also hail from the same stock, the same families, just a brief time lapse from the perpetrators. Much then of recent German thought was concerned with a necessary confrontation with a past that spilled over into the present, and offered so many devastating questions.

Some of the most interesting literature in Germany and beyond, that deals with the state of the nation, circles around what is known as 'Bewältigung der Vergangenheit', a collective description of the enterprise concerned with 'overcoming the past'.[5] Could a country which had piloted such a monstrous enterprise, and so recently too, be seen as normal? Or could it become normal? What sort of atonement is meaningful in such circumstances? All are involved. The perpetrators themselves, naturally. The bystanders too, who allowed it, and the others who could not adequately resist. The successor population too which presided over the absorption of those elements (and they must have been enormous, in view of what had happened) into the new Germany. And what of those born after the war, or who had been too young to have played any part in the events?

Of the many works which take up these themes, one of the most interesting and exciting is the hugely popular novel, *The Reader*, by Bernhard Schlink (b. 1944).[6] It is a story told in three parts by a first person narrator, whose life span seems to run closely parallel to the author's own. It opens with the narrator aged fifteen, and covers a period of some thirty five years. So it is a retrospective, bringing a relationship, which had dominated his early life and entered into his whole subsequent existence, into current perspective. As a youngster, he had grown up in an academic family, his father a Philosophy professor. The early setting, probably in 1959, in an unnamed Rhineland town, is carefully reconstructed.

---

[5] A slightly different term was earlier employed by Theodor Adorno as, for example, in his essay, 'Was bedeutet: Aufarbeitung der Vergangenheit', *Neues kritische Modelle* (Sührkamp, 1970) (based on a lecture originally delivered in 1954, and published in 1962). This formulation perhaps suggests 'working through' the past, rather than encountering it more vigorously.

[6] Bernhard Schlink, *Der Vorleser* (1995). *The Reader,* trans. Carol Brown Janeway (London: Phoenix, 1997).

The adolescent Michael is recovering from hepatitis, and is helped, when on a walk near his home, seized by an attack of vomiting, by the 36 year old Hanna Schmitz, he is taken into her home, cleaned up, and generally looked after. This leads to a sexual experience, and fascination on the part of Michael with the older woman. She instructs him in the ways of lovemaking, and this period of Michael's school career is dominated by his need to be with her on a regular basis. She, it transpires, works as a conductress on the buses, seems to have no family, and also has no ambition to progress to a more demanding career. This is the case, despite her own self-contempt, and other features which would seem to mark her out for something more. She dismisses her own life pattern, and insists that Michael devote himself seriously to his studies. His own confidence grows, partly as a result of the sexual mastery which he acquires, and also consequent upon his intellectual capacities. He becomes more independent and thoughtful, and is encouraged by his older mistress, who asks him to tell her of what he is learning, and asks him to read to her. This pattern is formative, and he becomes the 'reader'. But, coincidentally with his ongoing maturation and preoccupation with his now adult concerns, she suddenly leaves the city, and is apparently untraceable, both at home and at work.

Part 2 takes us forward seven years. Michael is a Law student, and one of their projects is to follow the course of the Law in relation to the crimes of the Third Reich. Coincidental with this, a trial is taking place locally, and Michael, together with the other students, are asked to follow the proceedings. Michael, in an estimate of himself and his contemporaries, concludes that: 'Our generation...subjected the parents' generation...to trial by daylight, and condemned it to shame.' (90) Hanna is one of the defendants. It transpires that she had joined the SS voluntarily, and eventually served in Auschwitz. Michael is led not only to ask questions of the accused, but also to direct such questions to himself: 'What should our second generation have done? What should it do with the knowledge of the horrors of the extermination of the Jews?' (102) The question reverberates throughout, just as Hanna's question redirected to the judge, strikes again, after the issue of her actions has been put to her: ' "[S]o what would you have done?" ' (110) She had been in charge of young girls, and had to make a 'selection' of who would be sent to the gas. She had apparently chosen especially weak girls for special attention, and asked them to 'read' to her, before they were sent for extermination. Michael asks of himself: 'Didn't she want to make the last days tolerable for weak girls?' (116) At the trial, when it comes to a question of who wrote the report (an issue which would have implied extra responsibility), she admits that it was she who had written it. At this point, the narrator suddenly realises that she was illiterate, a fact that would have explained her apparent reluctance to read anything herself in his company, as well as her unwillingness to apply for promotion at work. Even now, it seems that she prefers to admit to responsibilities that she could not have shouldered rather than to the shame of illiteracy. She receives a life sentence.

The third section of the novel takes us forward many years. Hanna has been in prison for eight years, when Michael decides to start sending her tapes of his 'readings'. He goes right through *The Odyssey* and passages from Schnitzler and Chekhov. This goes on for ten further years of imprisonment. In the meantime, Michael had had several further relationships, had married Gertrud, fathered a daughter, Julia, and then divorced. It seems that all later such relationships had taken place in the shadow of his earlier one with Hanna. Hanna is a permanently hovering memory. Of course, by the time of her release, she is an elderly woman. Michael's despatch of the tapes over the years had been known to the governess, who requests him, as Hanna's only known acquaintance to make arrangements for her reception back into the community. This he does. But, on the morning of her release, she is found hanged. She had committed suicide. She had left a note (in the meantime, she had taught herself to read and write) for Michael, and some money for the single survivor of a fire, where many women had been trapped, and for which she had been found responsible at the trial. Michael takes this money to the woman survivor, now in New York, and she decides that it should go to a foundation for Jewish illiterates.

The novel clearly revolves around the question of guilt and responsibility. Hanna had been guilty of the most horrific crimes; that was beyond doubt. But what of himself? Had he not loved a criminal? And had he not attempted to understand her? Can understanding and condemnation go together? He had guessed at her illiteracy, and yet had finally not intervened (his father's philosophical advice had tended against that sort of intervention, as being an intrusion into the free action of an adult). Can Michael's own generation afford to be complacent, or even exonerated? Are they not arrogant in their assumption of superior ethical standards, whereas, in fact, they must be of the same mould, even cut of the same cloth?

Between the Generations

There was so much history in the twentieth century, so many radical changes wrought, with the dramatically growing population, the changes in economic patterns, the mass emigrations, demographic realignments, the world wars, that it is not surprising that extra tensions were wrought between the generations. These came about in addition to what is standard in social patterns, when the successor generation acclimatises more naturally to

181

innovation and change. In Germany, this contrast is more marked than elsewhere. Not only had this country been in the vanguard of advanced technology and in national and cultural development, but it had also taken the most radical step backwards, reversing into an unprecedently primal barbarism. And then this phase was succeeded by a determined and hurried embrace of the cultural norms of post-war Europe, and the assumption of normality. Could there be such a radical separation over such a brief time span? It is no wonder then that those making an attempt to grasp the significance of these events and transitions have been locked in wonderment, and then pose questions to which there are apparently no unambiguous answers. The novel is a peculiarly appropriate vessel for the containment of the ongoing investigation into the nature of contemporary German society, and the way in which the present can come to terms with the past.

The Oxford born Rachel Seifert (b. 1971), denizen of Berlin, presents a portrait of generations in her novel, *The Dark Room*.[7] The three sections of the novel take us through three generations of separate German families. The first focuses on the life of Helmut in Berlin, born in 1921, growing up then with the rise of Nazism, although he, with an inherent physical defect in his right arm, is not drafted. The second section takes over the story with the German defeat. This is a tale of despair and flight, awaiting the enemy, only concerned that they should meet the American or British occupiers rather than the Russians, whom they fear above all. It is at this stage that the reports of German mass murders begin to filter through, uncensored. The third and main section takes us to what is virtually the present day, beginning in 1997, and follows the tortured consciousness of Micha.

---

[7] Rachel Seifert, *The Dark Room* (London: Vintage, 2002).

182

The novel's presentation is puzzling. Normally with the saga form we expect to follow a single family line or at least perceive an interconnected web. Here, no connection is made. The book could be seen as a series of discrete stories, except that the very precise time indicators tell us that we are dealing with a chronological mapping of what could be typical German reactions to the phenomenon of Nazism, before, during, and then in retrospect. We can see this in the authorial comment, early on in section one, in the third person account of Helmut: 'Puberty and the Third Reich arrive simultaneously.' (12) It is as though there is no clear division between the personal life as lived within by the central character, and the public event outside. They interlock, reflect on each other, and then become one. We then see these events and the interaction of Helmut with them from Helmut's own point of view. His parents have joined the Party, so his own ideals are shaped by the powerful familial, social and national norms imposed on him. His perspective, and, by extension, ours, is sharpened by the profession of photographer that he adopts whilst everyone else seems to be fighting and dying. The practice of this art and its description help us to view what is happening to Germany, which he views from the point of view of someone obsessed with trains and stations. He photographs a Berlin at war, which is a city emptying out. By 1945, the city has turned to rubble, and he can preside over it.

The early held assumptions of German superiority and inevitable victory are now brought into a strange focus with the reality of 1945, in the second section of the novel. A family is in flight on the way to Hamburg (within the British zone), but they first reach Nurenberg to meet up with their *Oma*. They are confronted simultaneously with absolute defeat, and knowledge of their war crimes, as there has been no surrender. Hitler had decided to fight to the end. Literally so, as this end was only marked by his own suicide, and the whole country is devastated. The proclaimed virtue of the Fatherland is counter pointed with the grim present. The action moves quickly, and the staccato prose style of the text matches this changing scene. The content here is factual, constructed of precise images as befits the eye of a camera, to which we became accustomed in the first section. The concerns, as registered in the dramatis personae, are primal, concerned with physical survival.

Section three takes up the staccato account, presenting the bare facts. In 1997, Micha is a teacher, who becomes a researcher into the recent German past. His wife, Mina, is of Turkish origin, although when confronted with the question of her identity as seen by herself, she describes herself, after much consideration, as German-Turkish rather than Turkish-German. The issue of identity is overriding here. Micha wants to examine the nature of his *Opa* and his activities in occupied Belarus. He investigates specifically the genocide carried out in the Minsk region in order to discover the part played there by his grandfather. He had been in the Waffen SS. Was he indeed Micha's *Opa* or a Nazi? How could one be both? How to hold two such apparently mutually preclusive identities together? That these can apparently coexist is a deeply troubling phenomenon. Micha has nightmares more resulting from films of a genial Hitler with his family than of Auschwitz. Micha has to resolve this conundrum in relation to his *Opa*, who is presumably part of his own identity, and he follows a trail to Belarus to find out more.

Micha is deeply troubled by what he discovers not only about the past, but about the present and its relation to that past. He is very angry, that at school commemorations, the children identify with the survivors: ' "They are being taught that there are no perpetrators, only victims" ' (290), he tells his wife. His obsession with the need to penetrate the truth, to discover the actual

184

events, takes him back to Belarus once more. His informant there is Kolesnik, a Belorussian (not a Jew, because all the Jews are dead), whom he sees, reasonably as a victim, who finds it difficult to return to that scene, and open out, particularly to a German. But it then transpires that Kolesnik, on his own confession, had been a collaborator. In regard to his father, there is no surviving record. But, Kolesnik had informed him he must have been a killer too. It would be naive to think otherwise: ' "That's what they were here for." ' (363) There were very few who resisted the order to kill, and it is they who are remembered for this protest. His *Opa* was not amongst these few. This activity must have been recorded in the letters that he had burned on his return from the front. Kolesnik dies, Micha hears, following his second return to Germany.

There seems to be no possible reconciliation or closure. Micha goes to Belarus once more, at the request of Kolesnik's widow, and he visits the grave. The evidence had been necessary; the memory, the testimony, the record, what survived and what did not, the reports. But there is nothing to be done beyond the recognition of the truth, and the coming to terms with it.

Another Angle

The recent past has been so shocking and perplexing that efforts have been made from all directions to come to terms with it, if not to understand what has happened, then perhaps to see it from another unexpected point, and so more clearly. One of the oddest and most original of these efforts was made by the British novelist, Martin Amis (b. 1949) in his novel, *Time's Arrow*.[8] This first person account, Part 1, opens in the USA of the present time, with the narrator, born, as we are to discover in 1916, paralysed. He arbitrarily moves backwards in time, apparently without realising it, taking it for granted that he seems to become younger and fitter. In order also to afford an alternative perspective to the narrative, he has an associate, Tod Friendly, a doctor, who is the narrator himself projected onto the outside, as he says: 'I am the hidden sharer of his body.' (64) The strangeness of the narrative direction does result in the shaking up of certainties in the way that events occur, and he can then subject his own perception to a sceptical line of enquiry: 'I'm getting more tentative about cause and effect' (52), he avers, and this uncertainty over order, what happens first, and why the sequence follows, naturally must communicate itself to the reader. But the setting becomes more specific as we move through the Vietnam war into the familiar landscape of World War II.

Several doubts must be raised in regard to the technique adopted. One such doubt touches on the overall objective. If time sequence is precisely reversed, then the same pattern of cause and effect surely takes place, only in reverse, and it is difficult to see how new insights might be obtained. Another problem is that if time is set in reverse, this can only be maintained with any meaningful consistency if each action also goes into reverse. Also, as the whole is filtered through the medium of language, then each sentence, each lexical item must also be reversed. Otherwise, we have the untenable situation that we are expected to view the scenario backwards, but then pause constantly in order to move in the forward direction in order to attend the exposition. It seems that it is

---

[8] Martin Amis, *Time's Arrow* (London: Penguin Books, 1992); orig. pub. by Jonathan Cape (London, 1991).

this kind of problematic that has made difficulties for the reader, posing not so much a reorientation of ethical and historical alignment, but rather an irritable reaching out for logic.

In any case, the experiment is amusing, and we find ourselves in New York, exchanging identities, seeing Tod Friendly's transformation into John Young. He (I) is a Nazi doctor, proclaiming his credo: 'The thing called society – It's behind us. We mediate between man and nature. We are the soldiers of a sacred biology.' (86) In fact, nothing is coherent: 'I keep expecting the world to make sense. It doesn't. It won't. Ever.' (91)

Part 2 of the novel takes us to Europe, firstly to 1948, awaiting a great war. Going through Italy, as the war's end, the finally arrives at Auschwitz, and it is here that he declares: 'The world is going to start making sense' (124), following the Bolsheviks' withdrawal (the story is of course unwinding in reverse). He is clearly a responsible operator of the crematoria, and he views the gassings, taking delight in the whole process: 'It is a common place to say that the triumph of Auschwitz was essentially organizational; we found the sacred fire that hides in the human heart – and built an autobahn that went there.' (132) The naked horror is clearly surveyed by the operator, and the reverse movement invests the act of gazing with shimmering irony. The reverse movement allows the impression that the 'victims' are resurrected for their return home, that, following the medical experiments, the patients become whole and healthy once more. The narrator too moves backward again, to his heyday in the Berlin of 1942, when he first went at the age of 25 to Auschwitz, that great cynosure of all Europe. He presents the death camp as a solution to the problem of the failure of the ghettos. Onwards, we see the narrator at the age of thirteen, touring in Poland, visiting Oswiecim and the wooded Birkenau, and then at the age of three, followed by the moment of birth, which came, (as the last words of the novel), '[e]ither too soon, or after it was all too late.' Thus is told '[t]he story of a man's life backward in time' (in *Time's Arrow*, Afterword, 175), quintessentially styled as a Nazi, in the terminology of the author, built like an autobahn that went to the core of the reptile brain, which, for him, is the specific 'nature of the offence'.

Auschwitz is Everything

A late convert to the view that the concentration camp experience has not only cast the rest of life into the shadows, but has rendered everything else meaningless, is the Hungarian writer, Imre Kertész (b. 1929), Nobel laureate in 2002. Following his deportation to Auschwitz and then Buchenwald and Zeitz (attached to Buchenwald), he returned, following the liberation, to attempt to resume normality in his native country. He made his living as an author of comedies and light journalism. But, in the wake of the collapse of the Communist regime in 1989, as well as of his own disillusionment with his original declared Socialistic sympathies, he recast himself as a Holocaust writer. He had already immersed himself once more in the nightmare world of the camps in his work, *Fateless*,[9] flagged as a novel, but presented in the first person under the fictional name of George Koves, and very close to autobiography. Later, he was to write: 'Nothing interests me really, only the myth of Auschwitz. Whatever I am thinking about, I am always thinking about Auschwitz ... I see everything else as imbecility in comparison to it.'[10] That incarceration served as an all consuming experience, turning him into a 'medium of Auschwitz',

---

[9] Imre Kertész, *Fateless* (Evanston: Northwestern Press, 1992); orig. pub. as *Sorstalanság* (Budapest, 1975).
[10] Imre Kertész, *Gályanapló* (Galley Diary), (Budapest, 1992), 36.

and transforming him into someone who has become, to some degree, a man who identifies with the murderers, and has a will to self-denial, hatred, and death. His later writing, which he regards as his authentic expression, is concerned with himself, and with his life and partial death in the Nazi camps.

In *Fateless*, we follow the fortunes of George and his family, from the moment that his father is 'conscripted into the labor service', and the disaster immediately unfolds, on this 'our dark, dark day', in the words of his stepmother. He is now in his fifteenth year. So we know from the author's own biography, which clearly serves as the template for the work, that we are talking about 1944, the year of the German takeover of Hungary, and the sealing of the fate of Hungarian Jewry. The reader is thus plunged straight into the horrific story without further ado or explanation. The presumption is that no such prologue is required, and the reader certainly knows where the action stands at this time and place. Presumably too, the actors themselves, in that scene thirty years removed from the time of composition (or, at least, of publication, as the book was many years in germination), also knew with virtual certainty what likely fate lay in store for them. There had already been considerable experience of the Nazi conquests and terror. But we see the events now through the eyes of the burgeoning adolescent.

The narrator presents a detailed and precise account of life, thoughts and feelings generated by the actual situation. The personal intertwines with the political. The father, who has hitherto been a successful merchant, is taken off to a 'labour camp', and the narrator has to step in as the responsible family head. As his uncle Lajos presses on him, he has become 'part of Jewish fate' (15), as tension reaches boiling point. But George insists on penetrating the reality and whatever lies behind it. He had little knowledge of matters Jewish; not of Jewish history, Jewish customs, practices, religion or languages. Raised as a marginal Jew, although sharing the inglorious lot of the race, he really wants to understand the meaning of the refrain that is also echoed in the title of the book, 'Fate', Jewish Fate. He learned that being Jewish carries the death penalty.[11] But his tone is cool, distant, curious and objectified, as though holding up the evidence and presenting it for examination, although he himself is a victim of this circumstance.

This detached tone is retained even in the presentation of his transport to Auschwitz, a name, he says, that he had hitherto not heard. The author captures the naïveté of the young narrator, as he gradually learns the truth of the reality of the camps. He is willing to embrace the technicalities of the distinctions made between an *Arbeitslager* (work camp) and a *Vernichtungslager* (extermination camp), between his brief stay at Auschwitz, which was of course evacuated in the face of the approaching Soviet army, and Buchenwald, close to Weimar. In Zeitz, Buchenwald, he observes his own speedily rotting body, as though detached from it. His shoes get stuck to his feet, and, in his own words, he approaches the state of becoming a 'Muslim', virtually dead in half-life. Following the liberation, when questioned by those curious, he says that he feels only hatred. But he is advised by his uncle to forget the past; ' "so that you may live." ' (186). But this is advice which he finds ludicrous, since the past is the reality, and can not be altered by one's will. In a sense though, he has found himself. He is the one who has lived out the 'fate' (188), although paradoxically, the notion of fate is the antithesis of freedom. But, for this, he has received a prize, which is, the license to live on.

The discovery made by Kertész is the determination to assess this life as given, and the only significant element in it, for

---

[11] Imre Kertész, *Kaddish for a Child not Born* (Evanston: Northwestern University Press, 1997), 17. Orig. pub. as, *Kaddis a meg nem született gyermekért* (Budapest: Magveto, 1990).

him. A further 'autobiographical novel', a long, single paragraph of a text, is *Kaddish for a Child not Born*.[12] More than a novel, this is a taking stock, an internal monologue, although it projects at least two interlocutors, the philosopher, Dr. Oblath, and his wife, now his ex-wife, who serves as a sounding board for his own speculations. As the title indicates, the narrator (this is also a first person account) reflects on what it means to be childless in a world that contained the Holocaust, in which it occurred, and, consequently then, where it could recur. He writes (he is a professional author and translator) because he must write. He quotes the view that, as long as there was a God, one had to conduct a dialogue with God. But now that He is dead, one must sustain a dialogue with other people, or, better still, with oneself. (15) And that is what he does in this book. He returns to the central theme of Fate, which he now describes as a series of recognitions. Analysis must be applied, rather than just retreat from the confrontation as from an irrational phenomenon beyond our cognition. Auschwitz can be explained, he implies by his strong rejection of simply regarding it as inexplicable. Throwing up one's hands in despair, he asserts, is an unworthy reaction. And his response is to write, as that is what he can and must do. There is a problem in the creation of literature though, and that is that books are doomed by their nature to repeat life, although they are fundamentally not life, and therefore fall short. (35) But there are serious connections, and these can be explored by the work of digging out, discovering the moment like an archaeologist. (39) That is the creative power of pain. (40) His writing, and thus, his existence, is an ongoing search for self-knowledge. Everything in his life has become part of a process, which is his fate, creating a meaningful entity, which he must struggle to recognise, in order to reject randomness. And he can

---

[12] Op. cit.

only plough this furrow. Commercial or popular success are not to the point, as he understands his trade; the work is its own purpose, and it is the discovery of himself. This leads him to the final rejection, articulated to the one who had been his wife, the rejection of the possibility of fathering a child. That child may claim to reject Jewishness, a Jewishness which means nothing to him as an abstraction, but which, as experience, means everything. (69) The work of the author is the existential acceptance of an imposed fate, a fact that is central to his life, and that becomes the theme of his literary work, which constitutes the expression of that life.

Summary

There are no easy conclusions to be drawn in regard to the range of fictions that has flourished around the Holocaust, except that the 'nature of the offence' has drawn to it an explosion of fictional enquiry and probing. This will no doubt continue, as creative writing must live as the instrument of such enquiry. It will surely adopt all the tools accessible to the human mind, and will help us to learn more from the ambition. This is not a process which has a conclusion. As we have seen, the experience of Auschwitz can be just as much the product of not having been in Auschwitz. Later generations relive, reexperience, and also rewrite that which has happened, and that which continues to happen.

IX

POSTSCRIPT: MEMORY, THE AUTHENTIC
AND THE APPOPRIATE

The Holocaust has been such a huge catalyst of literary reaction that any selection for presentation and analysis must, of necessity, be small and partial. So it is with the material presented
here. What we have shown does, I think, indicate, not only that the
pressure towards articulation of the experience was virtually immediate, but that it has continued up to the present day over a
great range of genres, cultures, countries and languages. This will
no doubt be the case in the future too, as the event was breathtak-
ing in its scope, and so challenging to what are regarded as normal
social and ethical norms. The Holocaust constitutes a moral
marker for the generations past and present, an event conducted
by human beings, and for that reason, demanding a human response of as great a variety and potential as can be articulated in
words.

The works and writers selected for analysis are to some
extent representative in typology and perspective. There are the
memoirs of victims and survivors. At some points they border on
the documentary, but they also at times transcend the actual
events, and exploit the freer range allowed by fictional form. But
here, the borderline between fact and fiction is often blurred, with

all the dangers inherent in such an enterprise. The work itself can clarify the nature of its own presentation, so that it does not trespass on foreign fields, and thus mislead the reader in his own search for truth. Truth is itself an ambiguous and complex notion, something to which we have much alluded in these discussions.

In the search for the truth of the experience, probably the ultimate is reached by the Austrian born, Jean Améry (1912-1978). Although in terms of Jewish Law he was not Jewish (his mother was a Catholic), he was so under the Nazi Nuremberg Laws. But, rather than reject that label, with all its dreadful implications he embraced it, in an existential rather than a religious sense. Both as an oppositionist who fled to Belgium, and more so, as a Jew, he was sent to Auschwitz, and somehow survived humiliation and torture. His writing beyond that point that point consisted of a meditation on those events, on Germany, on Nazism, and on his own identity. He changed his Germanic name, Hans Mayer, disguising the surname with the Gallicised anagram that he adopted. But he continued to write in German, expressing, as implied in the English translated title of his best-known book, the extreme of physical and mental experience.[1] He dismisses a notion that was becoming increasingly accepted in Liberal circles, that of shared experience, and thus, of moral equivalence. For him, the facts remain, hard as nuts, down to guilt and the impossibility of atonement. The only possibility left to all of us, victims, perpetrators, and others too, is the full recognition of what happened. On this we must all ponder, taking in the truth without self-delusion.

Beyond the generation contemporaneous with the events themselves is the so-called second generation, that generation which has borne the direct traces of the experience from their heri-

---

[1] Jean Améry, *At the Mind's Limits* trans. Sidney Rosenfeld and Stella P. Rosenfeld (Bloomington: Indiana University Press, 1980); orig. pub. as *Jenseits von Schuld und Sühne* (Stuttgart: Klett-Cotta, 1978).

tage, even, one might say, in its genes. This is so, not only on the part of the descendants of the victims, but on the part too, of the descendants of the 'other side', that of the perpetrators, the bystanders, or, at least, the cohort of the oppressors. All these groups constitute the people who seek out meaning and interpretation of their familial history, those who need to deal with a past that has close and urgent implications for the present. We have seen this not only in regard to the Germans, but in regard to writers from other countries as well. There are those who look to the Holocaust in order to seek out ways of drawing close to the subject, in sympathy or in wonderment. Then, there are writers who were not literally second generation of the victims or perpetrators, but who may have been close to that experience. There are those too who managed to get away, and to write from a distant shore, sometimes making a debut in Europe, but then continuing further afield, perhaps in Israel, in the USA, or in places as far afield as Australia.

The range of chapters here takes samples of such writing in the work of Ka-Tzetnik, a primary survivor, Kovner, a fighter poet, Liebrecht, a second generation writer in Israel, Grossman, of a later generation, imagining himself into the posture of a second generation writer, and reinventing himself as a young lad growing up in that atmosphere, Kosinski, the child survivor of a parallel nightmare experience, who got away to the USA and a different culture, and then Primo Levi, the archetypal presenter of the Lager, cool, apparently detached, and passionate, the authoritative voice of the concentrationary experience. In the first chapter, we have tried to indicate the parameters of this creative literature, and in the final chapter, we have offered some examples of later 'fictional' work deriving from the same source, and relating to its possible implications. This too is interesting for the range suggested, and possible lines for future exploration. Beyond the scope of the present work, there are so many other authors who are immediately relevant. There exists for example the problematic nature of a writer such as Binjamin Wilkomirski, who projected himself into the position of a victim, writing up the story a half century later, whose case has been extensively treated elsewhere.[2] Such a work bridges the genres of memoir and fiction, and its final status hangs on non-literary criteria. But the authentic and moving writings of Ida Fink still partake of the nature of both fiction and memoir. An immense host of important writers belongs to the almost limitless field of Holocaust literature. The field is so enormous because a whole world was affected, consciously or unconsciously. That world was transformed, both in its nature and in its assumptions, and any sort of life beyond is to be lived in the awareness of what took place during the fateful years of the Second World War. The subject has not been foreclosed here by any means, but, at the most, it has been opened up a little more, and awaits expansion and further exposition.

Memory, the Authentic and the Appropriate

The questions raised constantly recur. What is genuinely remembered? Is that element significant? Is that memory 'true'? And does it have to be objectively verifiable? What sort of memory are we talking about, is the question posed by Gillian Banner.[3] As the title of her book, and the authors treated indicate, the 'memory' spoken of there does not relate exclusively to past events. Neither, she suggests, does it have to work in the accepted, sequential fashion, with one event preceding another, and then

---

[2] See Leon Yudkin, *Public Crisis and Literary Response: The Adjustment of Modern Jewish Literature* (Paris: Suger Press, 2001).
[3] Gillian Banner, *Holocaust Literature: Schulz, Levi, Spiegelman and the Memory of the Offence* (London: Vallentine Mitchell, 2000).

followed by a line of connected elements. The memory spoken of is of what goes on in the mind, although of course it is related to the outer world, and may spring from the external catalyst: 'Survivor memory memorizes disconnectedness, not connectedness: the experiences encountered exist as distilled memory, unmediated by chronology, meaning, closure.' (28) Schulz puts together the past with the future. Levi, as we have seen, speaks of the unreliability of memory, and that memory changes and grows '[b]y incorporating extraneous features.'[4] The process dictates that: 'The distinction between the true and the false progressively loses its contours.' (14) We see then that memory has two facets; it is 'true'. But it also possesses its own momentum and direction.

It is also the case that, in the nature of the present story, this 'memory' will no longer be in the possession of survivors. It will have to be retained, shared, and passed on by others, 'raked up again' by memorialisation. These others are no longer the victims, the witnesses, or even, necessarily, the children of witnesses. The word will pass out of the control of the immediately involved parties, and the material presented will float freely. The subjects too will be presented for their appeal to the readership, one hungry for sensation, perhaps not approved by the arbiters of taste. As Gitta Sereny has observed: 'The people who commit crimes are unfortunately more interesting to the public than their victims.'[5] Bernstein has clearly preferred the use of what is now known as 'sideshadowing' rather than 'backshadowing', i.e. the preference of the author for allowing the actual options of the live character to be manifest at the point of the action, rather than the benefit of

---

[4] Primo Levi, *The Drowned and the Saved*, 11-12.
[5] Gitta Sereny, 'The Tragedy of Mary Bell; A Tale of Three Enduring Burdens', *The Times* (London, 24.5.2003).

hindsight.[6] It is not legitimate on the part of the author, who has total control of his material, to exploit the fact that he knows the outcome, to obtrude this superior knowledge over the players in the drama. We, unfortunately have knowledge of the fate of European Jewry. But does that grant us the right of a privileged view of those struggling in the arena before the disaster took place? Such use of anachronistic material must colour the authenticity of the representation. In any case, as James Young has pointed out, we, of a later generation, can only know events through what is passed down. It is on this basis that we see '[h]ow historical memory, understanding and meaning are constructed in Holocaust narrative.'[7] We have to be able to read the material in a manner appropriate to its nature: 'Several currents flow at differing depths in Holocaust testimonies, and that our understanding of the event depends very much on the source and destination of the current we pursue.'[8] And, as for the reliability of that memory, and of the effort of recovery, which might seem to cast doubt on its truth, again we have to go back to the sense that the mind now has its own story, and that story has been there from origin of its gestation. It may be very long after the event, but the source has never dried up, and it does not have to be brought to life. Langer asserts: 'I think the terminology is at fault here. There is no need to revive what has never died.'[9]

That material can make itself manifest, and be expressed long after the event is of course familiar from the work of Freud.

---

[6] Michael André Bernstein, *Foregone Conclusions: Against Apocalyptic History* (Berkeley Los Angeles: University of California Press, 1944).

[7] James Young, *Writing and Rewriting the Holocaust* (Bloomington: Indiana University Press, 1990), vii.

[8] Lawrence Langer, Holocaust Testimonies (New Haven: Yale University Press, 1991), xi.

[9] Op. cit., xv.

His use of the term 'latency' characterises the phenomenon of a trauma coming to the surface long after the shock that triggered it, as he discovered amongst patients suffering from shock trauma during the First World War. It is a noted phenomenon too that people can apparently survive a dreadful episode without apparently immediate distress, but experience nightmares and other disturbances long afterwards. What happens is that the patient relives the experience.[10] Holocaust literature can be usefully seen as a form of reliving the experience, even for those who were not involved directly. In a sense, we are all reliving the experience. The writer is the one putting the flesh, historiographical, personal, imagined, or conceived in whatever way, on an experience, that might be a memory or a fear, that is common to the human species.

---

[10] This phenomenon has been noted and analysed in Cathy Caruth, *Unclaimed Experience: Trauma, Narrative, and History* (Baltimore and London: The Johns Hopkins University Press, 1996).

BIBLIOGRAPHY

(Works referred to in the course of this book)

Adorno, T., 'Was bedeutet: Aufarbeitung der Vergangenheit', *Neues kritische Modelle* (Frankfurt am Main: Suhrkamp, 1970).

Améry, J., *At the Mind's Limits*, trans. Sidney Rosenfeld and Stella P. Rosenfeld (Bloomington: University of Indiana Press, 1980); orig. pub. as *Jenseits von Schuld und Sühne* (Stuttgart: Klett-Cotta, 1978).

Amis, M., *Time's Arrow* (London: Jonathan Cape, 1991; London: Penguin Book, 1992).

Aristotle, *On the Art of Poetry*, trans. from Greek Ingram Bywater. (London: Oxford University Press, 1959).

Banner, G., *Holocaust Literature: Schulz, Levi, Spiegelman, and the Memory of the Offence* (London: Vallentine Mitchell, 2000).

Bartov, O., 'Kitsch and Sadism in Ka-Tsetnik's Other Planet: Israeli Youth Imagine the Holocaust', *Jewish Social Studies*, vol.3, no.2 (1997), 42-76.

Bernstein, M. A., *Foregone Conclusions: Against Apocalyptic History* (Berkeley: University of California Press, 1994).

Borowski, T., *This Way to the Gas, Ladies and Gentlemen,* trans. from Polish by Barbara Vedder (New York: Viking, 1967).

Caruth, C., *Unclaimed Experience: Trauma, Narrative, and History* (Baltimore: The Johns Hopkins University Press, 1996).

Ezrahi, S. D., *By Words Alone* (Chicago: The University of Chicago Press, 1975).

Fink, I., *A Scrap of Time*, trans. from Polish Madeline Levine and Francine Prose (New York: Schocken Modern Classics, 1987).

Grossman, D., *Rats: Stories* (Tel Aviv: Siman qriah, 1983).

—— *Hiyukg ha-gdi* (Tel Aviv: Siman qriah, 1983).

—— *Ayen erekh: ahavah* (Tel Aviv: Siman qriah, 1986).

—— *Gan riqi. A play* (Tel Aviv: Siman qriah, 1988).

—— *Sefer ha-diqduq ha-pnimi* (Tel Aviv: Siman qriah, 1991).

—— *Nokhahim nifqadim* (Tel Aviv: Siman qriah, 1992).

—— *Yesh yeladim zigzag* (Tel Aviv: Siman qriah, 1997).

—— *Shetihyi li ha-sakin* (Tel Aviv: Siman qriah, 1998).

—— *Mishehu laruts ito* (Tel Aviv: Siman qriah, 2000).

Kafka, F., *Letters to Felice* (London: Penguin Modern Classics, 1975).

Kaplan, C., *Scroll of Agony: The Warsaw Diary of Chaim Kaplan*, trans. from Hebrew and ed. Abraham Katsh. (New York: Macmillan, 1965).

Ka-Tzetnik 135633 (Yehiel Feiner). *Salamandra*, trans. from a Yiddish manuscript Y. L. Baruch (Tel Aviv: Shikmona, 1946).

—— *Bet ha-bubot* (Tel Aviv: Ha-qibuts ha-meuhad, 1953). Yiddish version *Dos hoyz fun di lialkes* (Buenos Aires: Shikhmona, 1955).

—— *Ha-shaon asher me-'al la-rosh* (Jerusalem: Mosad Bialik, 1960; 1972).

—— *Qaru lo pipel* (Tel Aviv: Ha-qibuts ha-meuhad, 1961)

—— *Ka-khol me-efer.* (Tel Aviv: Ha-qibuts ha-meuhad, 1966).

—— *Salamandra* (2nd ed. Tel Aviv: Ha-qibuts ha-meuhad, 1971). Published together with *Ha-imut* (*The Confrontation*), a retitled issue of *Ka-khol me-efer*, in one volume.

—— *Ha-shaon* (Jerusalem: Mosad Bialik. 1972).

—— *Der zayger vos uberen kop* (Tel Aviv: I. L. Perets, 1961).

—— *Di zeung* (Tel Aviv: I. L. Perets, 1990). (Includes 'Tsofen: a.dm.a.')

(Ka-Tzetnik translations into English)

—— *Sunrise over Hell*, trans. from Hebrew [*Salamandra*] Nina De-Nur (London: W. H. Allen, 1977).

—— *House of Dolls*, trans. from Hebrew [*Bet ha-bubot*] Moshe M. Kohn (New York: Simon and Schuster, 1955).

—— *Star Eternal*, translated from Hebrew [*Ha-shaon asher me-'al la-rosh*] Nina De-Nur (New York: Arbor House, 1971).

—— *They Called Him Piepel*, trans. from Hebrew [*Qaru lo pipel*] Nina De-Nur (London: Anthony Blond, 1961).

—— *Phoenix Over the Galilee*, trans. from Hebrew [*Ka-khol me-efer*] Nina De-Nur (New York: Harper, 1969).

—— *Shiviti: A Vision*, trans. from Hebrew [*Shiviti*] Eliya (Nina) De-Nur and Lisa Herman (New York: Harper and Row, 1989).

—— *Kaddish* (New York: Algemeiner Associates, 1998). (A collection of writings compiled together with Eliya (Nina) De-Nur, who had died on February 14, 1992.)

Kertész, I., *Fateless* trans. Christopher C. Wilson and Katharina M. Wilson (Evanston: Northwestern University Press, 1992); orig. pub. as *Sorstalanság* (Budapest: Magveto, 1975).

——— *Kaddish for a Child not Born*, trans. Christopher C. Wilson and Katharina M. Wilson (Evanston: Northwestern University Press, 1997); orig. pub. as *Kaddis a meg nem született gyermekért* (Budapest, 1990).

Kosinski, J., *The Painted Bird* (London: W. H. Allen, 1966; London: Corgi Books, 1966).

——— *Steps* (London: Bodley Head, 1969; Corgi Books, 1970).

——— *Being There* (London: Corgi Books, 1970).

——— *The Devil Tree* (London: Arrow Books, 1973).

——— *Cockpit* (London: Arrow Books, 1975).

——— *Blind Date* (Boston: Houghton Miffin Company, 1977).

——— *Passion Play* (New York: St. Martin's Press, 1979).

——— *Pinball* (London: Arrow Books, 1982).

——— *Passing By: Selected Essays, 1962-1991* (New York: Random House, 1992; Paperback edn. New York: Grove Press, 1995).

——— *The Future is Ours, Comrade* (An essay on Communism) (London: The Bodley Head, 1960).

Kovner, A., *Kol shirey aba qovner*, 3 vols. (Jerusalem: Mosad Bialik, 1996).

——— *Ahoti qtanah* (Tel Aviv: Sifriyat Poalim, 1967; 2nd edn. 1970).

——— *A Canopy in the Desert: Selected Poems by Abba Kovner*, trans. from Hebrew Shirley Kaufman, Ruth Adler and Nurit Orchan (Pittsburgh: University of Pittsburgh Press, 1973). (Including complete translation of *My Little Sister*).

——— *Shirat Roza* (Tel Aviv: Sifriyat Poalim, 1975; 2nd edn. 1987).

——— *Salon qetering* (Tel Aviv: Ha-qibuts ha-meuhad, 1987).

—— *Panim el panim*. 2 vols: 1. *She'at ha-efes*. 2. *Ha-tsomet* (Tel Aviv: Sifriyat Poalim, 1955).

Langer, L., *The Holocaust and the Literary Imagination* (New Haven: Yale University Press, 1975).

—— *Holocaust Testimonies* (New Haven: Yale University Press, 1991).

Lavers, N., *Jerzy Kosinski* (New York: Bantam Books, 1982).

Levi, P., *Se questo è un uomo* (Torino: Giulio Einaudi, 1958) (first pub. 1947). *If This is a Man*, translated from Italian Stuart Woolf (London: Orion Press, 1959; Penguin Press, 1993). Also pub. as *Survival in Auschwitz* in 1961.

—— *I sommersi e i salvati* (Torino: Giulio Einaudi, 1986). *The Drowned and the Saved*, trans. from Italian Raymond Rosenthal (London: Michael Joseph, 1988; Abacus, 1988).

—— *Il sistema periodico* (Torino: Giulio Einaudi, 1975). *The Periodic Table* (London: Michael Joseph, 1985).

Liebrecht, S., *Tapuhim min ha-midbar* (Tel Aviv: Sifriyat Poalim, 1986; New edn. Jerusalem: Keter, 1992).

—— *Sinit ani medaberet elekha* (Jerusalem: Keter, 1992).

—— *Susim 'al kvish gehah* (Tel Aviv: Kineret, 1988; New edn. Jerusalem: Keter, 1992).

—— *Tsarikh sof le-sipur ahavah* (Jerusalem: Keter, 1995).

—— *Ish ve-ishah ve-ish* (Jerusalem: Keter, 1998).

—— *Nashim mitokh qatalog* (Jerusalem: Keter, 2000).

—— *Apples from the Desert: Selected Stories*, Introduction by Lily Rattok (London: Loki Books, 1998).

Lilly, P., *Words in Search of Victims: The Achievement of Jerzy Kosinski*

(Kent: The Kent State University Press, 1988).

Lind, J., *Soul of Wood,* trans. from German Ralph Manheim. (London: Jonathan Cape, 1964); orig. pub. as *Eine Seele aus Holz* (Berlin, 1962).

Luria, S. (ed.) *Aba kovner; mivhar maamarey biqoret 'al yetsirato* (Tel Aviv: Ha-qibuts ha-meuhad, 1988).

Lustig, A., *Diamonds of the Night,* trans. From Czech Jeanne Némcova (London: Quartet Books, 1989); orig. pub. as *Démanty noci*, Prague, 1958.

Patterson, D., Alan Berger and Sarita Cargas (eds.) *Encyclopaedia of Holocaust Literature* (Wesport Ct.: Oryx Press, 2002).

Peli, M., 'Ha-bituy ha-omanuti shel sifrut ha-shoah nusakh ka-tsetnik', *Mahut*, vol.2, no.7 (1991), 148-159.

Popkin, J. D., 'Ka-Tzetnik 135633: The Survivor as Pseudonym'. *New Literary History*, vol.33.2, The University of Virginia (2002), 343-355.

Ringelbaum, E., *Notes from the Warsaw Ghetto,* trans. from Yiddish and ed. by Jacob Sloan (New York: McGraw-Hill, 1958).

Rosenberg, A., *A Double Dying: Reflections on Holocaust Literature* (Bloomington: Indiana University Press, 1980).

Rousset, D., *L'univers Concentrationnaire* (Paris: Le Pavois, 1947).

—— *L'institution Concentrationnaire en Russie (1930-1957)* (Paris: Plon, 1959).

Rudolf, A., 'Obituary' (Ka-Tsetnik), *The Independent* (27.7.2001), 6.

Schlink, B., *The Reader,* trans. from German Carol Brown Janeway (London: Phoenix, 1997); first pub. as *Der Vorleser.* Diogenes Verlag (Zürich, 1995).

Seifert, R., *The Dark Room* (London: Vintage Books, 2002).

Sereny, G., 'The Tragedy of Mary Bell: A Tale of Three Enduring Burdens', *The Times* (London, 24.5.2003).

Sheintukh, Y., 'Kitvey ka-tsetnik be-'esrim ha-shanim a-akhronot', *Dapim leheqer tequfat ha-shoah*, vol.14 (1997), 109-148.

—— 'e.d.m.'a: le-verur musag mafteah be-khitvey ka-tsetnik', *Hulyot*, vol.5 (1995), 275-290.

—— 'mif'al hantsahah shel adam ekhad: hitqablut ha-roman salamandra 'al-pi ha-biqoret ha-artsyisre-elit, 1946-7', *Dapim le-heqer tequfat ha-shoah*, vol.16 (1991), 143-166.

Sloane, J. P., *Jerzy Kosinski: A Biography* (New York: Dutton, 1996).

Steiner, G., *Language and Silence* (New York: Atheneum. 1966).

Styron, W., *Sophie's Choice* (London: Jonathan Cape, 1979; Corgi Books, 1981).

Thomas, D. M., *The White Hotel* (London: Penguin Books, 1981).

Wiesel, E., 'Jewish Values in the Post-Holocaust Future', *Judaism 16*, 1967.

—— *Legends of Our Time*, trans. from French Steven Donadio (New York: Holt, Reinhart and Winston, 1968).

Wistrich, R., *Who's Who in Nazi Germany* (London: Weidenfeld and Nicolson, 1982).

Young, J., *Writing and Rewriting the Holocaust: Narrative and the Consequences of Interpretation* (Bloomington: Indiana University Press, 1988).

Yudkin, L., *Public Crisis and Literary Response* (Paris: Suger, 2001).

Zylberberg, M., *A Warsaw Diary, 1939-1945* (London: Vallentine Mitchell, 1969).

INDEX

(When subject headings constitute integral part of the individual chapters, they are not indexed separately.)